HF304314

Defoe Abbott Marx Hardy Melville Montaigne Machiavelli Haggard Emerson Chesterton Cooper Joyce Austen Hugo Eliot Grimm
Stoker Carroll Christie Maupassant Byron Molière Schiller
Wilde Garnett Einstein Fitzgerald Engels Smith Kafka Hall
Goethe Hawthorne Dostoyevsky Kipling Doyle Willis
Baum Cotton Henry Nietzsche Balzac
Leslie Dumas Flaubert Turgenev Crane
Stockton Vatsyayana Verne Vinci
Burroughs Curtis Tocqueville Gogol Busch
Homer Widger Tolstoy Whitman
Darwin Thoreau Twain Scott
Potter Freud Zola Lawrence Plato Harte
Kant Jowett Stevenson Dickens Burton Hesse
Andersen Cervantes
London Descartes Voltaire Cooke
Poe Aristotle Wells Hale James Hastings Irving
Bunner Shakespeare Chambers
Richter Chekhov da Benedict Alcott
Doré Dante Shaw Wodehouse Pushkin
Swift Newton

 **tredition®**

tredition was established in 2006 by Sandra Latusseck and Soenke Schulz. Based in Hamburg, Germany, tredition offers publishing solutions to authors and publishing houses, combined with world-wide distribution of printed and digital book content. tredition is uniquely positioned to enable authors and publishing houses to create books on their own terms and without conventional manufacturing risks.

For more information please visit: www.tredition.com

TREDITION CLASSICS

This book is part of the TREDITION CLASSICS series. The creators of this series are united by passion for literature and driven by the intention of making all public domain books available in printed format again - worldwide. Most TREDITION CLASSICS titles have been out of print and off the bookstore shelves for decades. At tredition we believe that a great book never goes out of style and that its value is eternal. Several mostly non-profit literature projects provide content to tredition. To support their good work, tredition donates a portion of the proceeds from each sold copy. As a reader of a TREDITION CLASSICS book, you support our mission to save many of the amazing works of world literature from oblivion. See all available books at www.tredition.com.

Project Gutenberg

The content for this book has been graciously provided by Project Gutenberg. Project Gutenberg is a non-profit organization founded by Michael Hart in 1971 at the University of Illinois. The mission of Project Gutenberg is simple: To encourage the creation and distribution of eBooks. Project Gutenberg is the first and largest collection of public domain eBooks.

Minnesota and Dacotah

Christopher Columbus Andrews

Imprint

This book is part of TREDITION CLASSICS

Author: Christopher Columbus Andrews
Cover design: Buchgut, Berlin – Germany

Publisher: tredition GmbH, Hamburg - Germany
ISBN: 978-3-8424-4403-4

www.tredition.com
www.tredition.de

Copyright:
The content of this book is sourced from the public domain.

The intention of the TREDITION CLASSICS series is to make world literature in the public domain available in printed format. Literary enthusiasts and organizations, such as Project Gutenberg, worldwide have scanned and digitally edited the original texts. tredition has subsequently formatted and redesigned the content into a modern reading layout. Therefore, we cannot guarantee the exact reproduction of the original format of a particular historic edition. Please also note that no modifications have been made to the spelling, therefore it may differ from the orthography used today.

MINNESOTA AND DACOTAH:

IN

Letters descriptive of a Tour through the North-West,

IN THE AUTUMN OF 1856.

WITH

INFORMATION RELATIVE TO PUBLIC LANDS,

AND

A TABLE OF STATISTICS.

By C. C. ANDREWS,

COUNSELOR AT LAW; EDITOR OF THE OFFICIAL OPINIONS OF THE ATTORNEYS GENERAL OF THE UNITED STATES.

"From the forests and the prairies,
 From the great lakes of the Northland,
 From the land of the Ojibways,
 From the land of the Dacotahs."

LONGFELLOW

SECOND EDITION.
W A S H I N G T O N:
ROBERT FARNHAM
1857

PHILADELPHIA:

STEREOTYPED BY E. B. MEARS.

PRINTED BY C. SHERMAN & SON.

THESE

"Trivial Fond Records"

ARE

RESPECTFULLY INSCRIBED

TO THE

YOUNG MEN OF MINNESOTA.

INTRODUCTION.

THE object of publishing these letters can be very briefly stated.

During the last autumn I made a tour into Minnesota, upwards of a hundred and thirty miles north-west of St. Paul, to satisfy myself as to the character and prospects of the territory. All I could learn from personal observation, and otherwise, concerning its society and its ample means of greatness, impressed me so favorably as to the advantages still open to the settler, that I put down in the form of letters such facts as I thought would be of general interest. Since their publication— in the *Boston, Post*— a few requests, which I could not comply with, were made for copies of them all. I was led to believe, therefore, that if I revised them and added information relative to unoccupied lands, the method of preemption, and the business interests of the territory, they would be worthy of publication in a more permanent form. Conscious that what I have written is an inadequate description of that splendid domain, I shall be happy indeed to have contributed, in ever so small a degree, to advance its growth and welfare.

Here I desire to acknowledge the aid which has been readily extended to my undertaking by the Delegate from Minnesota— Hon. HENRY M. RICE— whose faithful and unwearied services— I will take the liberty to add— in behalf of the territory, merit the highest praise. I am also indebted for valuable information to EARL S. GOODRICH, Esq., editor of the *Daily Pioneer* (St. Paul) *and Democrat.*

In another place I give a list of the works which I have had occasion to consult or refer to.

C. C. ANDREWS.

Washington, January 1, 1857.

LIST OF WORKS WHICH HAVE BEEN CONSULTED OR REFERRED TO IN THE PREPARATION OF THIS WORK.

Expedition to the Sources of the Mississippi, by Major Z. M. PIKE vol. Philadelphia; 1807.

Travels to the Source of the Missouri River, by Captains LEWIS and CLARKE. 3 vols. London: 1815.

Expedition to the Source of the St. Peter's River, Lake Winnepek, &c., under command of Major STEPHEN H. LONG 2 vols. Philadelphia: 1824.

British Dominions in North America. By JOSEPH BOUCHETTE, Esq. 3 vols. London: 1832.

History of the Colonies of the British Empire. By R. M. MARTIN, Esq. London; 1843.

Report on the Hydrographical Basin of the Upper Mississippi, by J. N. NICOLLET. Senate Document 237, 2d Session, 26th Congress. Washington: 1843.

Report, of an Exploration of the Territory of Minnesota, by Brevet Captain JOHN POPE, Corps Topographical Engineers. Senate Document 42, 1st Session, 31st Congress. Washington: 1850.

Sketches of Minnesota. By E. S. SEYMOUR. New York: 1850.

Report on Colonial and Lake Trade, by ISRAEL D. ANDREWS, Consul General of the United States for the British Provinces. Executive Document 112, 1st Session, 32d Congress. Washington: 1852.

History of the Discovery and Exploration of the Mississippi River. By J. G. SHEA. New York: 1852.

Minnesota and its Resources. By J. WESLEY BOND. New York: 1853.

Discovery of the Sources of the Mississippi River. By HENRY R. SCHOOLCRAFT. Philadelphia: 1855.

Exploration and Surveys for a Railroad Route from the Mississippi River to the Pacific Ocean, made under the direction of the Secretary of War in 1853-4, (including Reports of Gov. Stevens and others.) Washington: 1855.

The Emigrant's Guide to Minnesota By an Old Resident. 1 vol. St. Anthony: 1856.

CONTENTS.

LETTER I. BALTIMORE TO CHICAGO.

Anecdote of a preacher— Monopoly of seats in the cars— Detention in the night— Mountain scenery on the Baltimore and Ohio Railroad— Voting in the cars— Railroad refreshments— Political excitement— The Virginian and the Fremonters— A walk in Columbus— Indianapolis— Lafayette— Michigan City— Chicago

LETTER II. CHICAGO TO ST. PAUL.

Railroads to the Mississippi— Securing passage on the steamboat— The Lady Franklin— Scenery of the Mississippi— Hastings— Growth of settlements

LETTER III. CITY OF ST. PAUL.

First settlement of St. Paul— Population— Appearance of the city— Fuller House— Visitors— Roads— Minneapolis— St. Anthony— Suspension Bridge

LETTER IV. THE BAR.

Character of the Minnesota bar— Effect of connecting land business with practice— Courts— Recent Legislation of Congress as to the territorial judiciary— The code of practice— Practice in land cases— Chances for lawyers in the West— Charles O'Connor— Requisite qualifications of a lawyer— The power and usefulness of a great lawyer— Talfourd's character of Sir William Follett— Blending law with politics— Services of lawyers in deliberative assemblies

LETTER V. ST. PAUL TO CROW WING IN TWO DAYS.

Stages— Roads— Rum River— Indian treaty— Itasca— Sauk Rapids— Watab at midnight— Lodging under difficulties— Little Rock River— Character of Minnesota streams— Dinner at Swan River— Little Falls— Fort Ripley— Arrival at Crow Wing

LETTER VI. THE TOWN OF CROW WING.

Scenery— First Settlement of Crow Wing— Red Lake Indians— Mr. Morrison— Prospects of the town— Upper navigation— Mr. Beaulieu— Washington's theory as to Norfolk— Observations on the growth of towns

LETTER VII. CHIPPEWA INDIANS— HOLE-IN-THE-DAY.

Description of the Chippewa tribes— Their habits and customs— Mission at Gull Lake— Progress in farming— Visit to Hole-in-the-day— His enlightened character— Reflections on Indian character, and the practicability of their civilization— Their education— Mr. Manypenny's exertions

LETTER VIII. LUMBERING INTERESTS.

Lumber as an element of wealth— Quality of Minnesota lumber— Locality of its growth— The great pineries— Trespasses on government land— How the lumbermen elude the government— Value of lumber— Character of the practical lumberman— Transportation of lumber on rafts

LETTER IX. SHORES OF LAKE SUPERIOR.

Description of the country around Lake Superior— Minerals— Locality of a commercial city— New land districts— Buchanan— Ojibeway— Explorations to the sources of the Mississippi— Henry R. Schoolcraft— M. Nicollet's report— Resources of the country above Crow Wing

LETTER X. VALLEY OF THE RED RIVER OF THE NORTH.

Climate of Minnesota— The settlement at Pembina— St. Joseph— Col. Smith's expedition— Red River of the North— Fur trade— Red River Settlement— The Hudson's Bay Company— Ex-Gov. Ramsey's observations— Dacotah

LETTER XI. THE TRUE PIONEER.

Energy of the pioneer— Frontier life— Spirit of emigration— Advantages to the farmer in moving West— Advice in regard to making preemption claims— Abstract of the preemption law— Hints to the settler— Character and services of the pioneer

LETTER XII. SPECULATION AND BUSINESS.

Opportunities to select farms— Otter Tail Lake— Advantages of the actual settler over the speculator— Policy of new states as to taxing non-residents— Opportunities to make money— Anecdote of Col. Perkins— Mercantile business— Price of money— Intemperance— Education— The free school

LETTER XIII. CROW WING TO ST. CLOUD.

Pleasant drive in the stage— Scenery— The past— Fort Ripley Ferry— Delay at the Post Office— Belle Prairie— A Catholic priest— Dinner at Swan River— Potatoes— Arrival at Watab— St. Cloud

LETTER XIV. ST. CLOUD— THE PACIFIC TRAIL.

Agreeable visit at St. Cloud— Description of the place— Causes of the rapid growth of towns— Gen. Lowry— The back country— Gov. Stevens's report— Mr. Lambert's views— Interesting account of Mr. A. W. Tinkham's exploration

LETTER XV. ST. CLOUD TO ST. PAUL.

Importance of starting early— Judge Story's theory of early rising— Rustic scenery— Horses and mules— Surveyors— Humboldt— Baked fish— Getting off the track— Burning of hay stacks— Supper at St. Anthony— Arrival at the Fuller House

LETTER XVI. PROGRESS.

Rapid growth of the North-West— Projected railroads— Territorial system of the United States— Inquiry into the cause of Western progress— Influence of just laws and institutions— Lord Bacon's remark

THE PROPOSED NEW TERRITORY OF DACOTAH.

Organization of Minnesota as a state— Suggestions as to its division— Views of Captain Pope— Character and resources of the new territory to be left adjoining— Its occupation by the Dacotah Indians— Its organization and name

POST OFFICES AND POSTMASTERS

LAND OFFICES AND LAND OFFICERS

NEWSPAPERS PUBLISHED IN MINNESOTA

TABLE OF DISTANCES

PRE-EMPTION FOR CITY OR TOWN SITES

PART I.

LETTERS ON MINNESOTA.

MINNESOTA AND DACOTAH.

LETTER I.

BALTIMORE TO CHICAGO.

Anecdote of a preacher— Monopoly of seats in the cars— Detention in the night— Mountain scenery on the Baltimore and Ohio Railroad— Voting in the cars— Railroad refreshments— Political excitement— The Virginian and the Fremonters— A walk in Columbus— Indianapolis— Lafayette— Michigan City— Chicago.

CHICAGO, October, 1856.

I SIT down at the first place where a pen can be used, to give you some account of my trip to Minnesota. And if any one should complain that this is a dull letter, let me retain his good-will by the assurance that the things I expect to describe in my next will be of more novelty and interest. And here I am reminded of a good little anecdote which I am afraid I shall not have a better chance to tell. An eminent minister of the Gospel was preaching in a new place one Sunday, and about half through his sermon when two or three dissatisfied hearers got up to leave, "My friends," said he, "I have one small favor to ask. As an attempt has been made to prejudice my reputation in this vicinity, I beg you to be candid enough, if any one asks how you liked my sermon, to say you didn't stop to hear me through."

Stepping into the cars on the Baltimore and Ohio Railroad a few evenings ago— for I am not going to say anything of my trip further east— I saw as great an exhibition of selfishness as one often meets in travelling. This was in the rear car, the others being all crowded. The seats were spacious, and had high backs for night travelling. A gentleman entered the car and proposed to sit in a seat in which was only one child, but he was informed by a feminine voice in the rear that the whole seat was taken— so he advanced to the next seat, which was occupied by another child, a boy about eight years old— again the same voice, confirmed by one of the other sex, informed him in very decided terms that that also was wholly occupied. The gentleman of course did not attempt to take a seat with this lady, but advancing still further, in a seat behind her he saw another child the only occupant. His success here was no better. The fact was, here was a family of a husband, wife, and three children occupying five entire seats. The traveller politely asked if it would not be convenient for two of the children to sit together. "No," said the lady and her husband (and they spoke together, though they didn't sit together), "the children want all the room so as to sleep." The traveller betrayed no feeling until the husband aforesaid pointed out for him a seat next to a colored woman who sat alone near the door of the car, some little distance off. It was quite apparent, and it was the fact, that this colored woman was the servant of the family; and the traveller appeared to think that, although as an "original question" he might not object to the proffered seat, yet it was not civil for a man to offer him what he would not use himself. The scene closed by the traveller's taking a seat with another gentleman, I mention this incident because it is getting to be too common for people to claim much more room than belongs to them, and because I have seen persons who are modest and unused to travelling subjected to considerable annoyance in consequence. Moreover, conductors are oftentimes fishing so much after popularity, that they wink at misconduct in high life.

Somewhere about midnight, along the banks of the Potomac, and, if I remember right, near the town of Hancock, the cars were detained for three hours. A collision had occurred twelve hours before, causing an extensive destruction of cars and freight, and heavy fragments of both lay scattered over the track. Had it not been for the skilful use of a steam-engine in dragging off the ruins, we must have waited till the sun was up. Two or three large fires were kindled with the ruins, so that the scene of the disaster was entirely visible. And the light shining in the midst of the thick darkness, near the river, with the crowd of people standing around, was not very romantic, perhaps not picturesque— but it was quite novel; and the novelty of the scene enabled us to bear with greater patience the gloomy delay.

The mountain scenery in plain sight of the traveller over the Baltimore and Ohio road is more extensive and protracted, and I think as beautiful, as on any road in the United States. There are as wild places seen on the road across Tennessee from Nashville, and as picturesque scenes on the Pennsylvania Central road— perhaps the White Mountains as seen from the Atlantic and St. Lawrence road present a more sublime view— but I think on the road I speak of, there is more gorgeous mountain scenery than on any other. On such routes one passes through a rude civilization. The settlements are small and scattered, exhibiting here and there instances of thrift and contentment, but generally the fields are small and the houses in proportion. The habits of the people are perhaps more original than primitive. It was along the route that I saw farmers gathering their corn on sleds. The cheerful scene is often witnessed of the whole family— father, mother, and children— at work gathering the crops. These pictures of cottage life in the mountain glens, with the beautiful variegated foliage of October for groundwork, are objects which neither weary nor satiate our sight.

The practice of taking a vote for presidential candidates in the cars has been run into the ground. By this I mean that it has been carried to a ridiculous excess. So far I have had occasion to vote several times. A man may be indifferent as to expressing his vote when out of his state; but a man's curiosity must have reached a high pitch when he travels through a train of cars to inquire how the passengers vote. It is not uncommon, I find, for people to carry out the joke by voting with their real opponents. Various devices are resorted to to get a unanimous vote. For example, a man will say, "All who are in favor of Buchanan take off their boots; all in favor of Fremont keep them on." Again, when there are several passengers on a stage-coach out west, and they are passing under the limbs of a tree, or low bridge, as they are called, it is not unusual far a Fremont man to say, "All in favor of Fremont bow their heads."

I have a word to say about refreshments on railroad routes. It is, perhaps, well known that the price for a meal anywhere on a rail-road in the United States is fifty cents. That is the uniform price. Would that the meals were as uniform! But alas! a man might as well get a quid of tobacco with his money, for he seldom gets a *quid pro quo*. Once in a couple of days' travel you may perhaps get a wholesome meal, but as a general thing what you get (when you get out of New England) isn't worth over a dime. You stop at a place, say for breakfast, after having rode all night. The conductor calls out, "Twenty minutes for breakfast." There is a great crowd and a great rush, of course. Well, the proprietor expects there will be a crowd, and ought to be prepared. But how is it? Perhaps you are lucky enough to get a seat at the table. Then your chance to get something to eat is as one to thirteen: for as there is nothing of any consequence on the table, your luck depends on your securing the services of a waiter who at the same time is being called on by about thirteen others as hungry as yourself. Then suppose you succeed! First comes a cup of black coffee, strong of water; then a piece of tough fried beef steak, some fried potatoes, a heavy biscuit— a little sour (and in fact everything is sour but the pickles). You get up when you have finished eating— it would be a mockery to say when you have satisfied your appetite— and at the door stand two muscular men (significantly the proprietor is aware of the need of such) with bank bills drawn through their fingers, who are prepared to receive your 50c. It is not unusual to hear a great deal of indignation expressed by travellers on such occasions. No man has a right to grumble at the fare which hospitality sets before him. But when he buys a dinner at a liberal price, in a country where provisions are abundant, he has a right to expect something which will sustain life and health. Those individuals who have the privilege of furnishing meals to railroad travellers probably find security in the reflection that their patronage does not depend on the will of their patrons. But the evil can be remedied by the proprietors and superintendents of the roads, and the public will look for a reformation in dinners and suppers at their hands.

I might say that from Benwood, near Wheeling— where I arrived at about four in the afternoon, having been nearly twenty-four hours coming 875 miles— I passed on to Zanesville to spend the night; thinking it more convenient, as it surely was, to go to bed at eleven at night and start the next morning at eight, than to go to bed at Wheeling at nine, or when I chose, and start again at two in the morning. The ride that evening was pleasant. The cars were filled with lusty yeomen, all gabbling politics. There was an overwhelming majority for Fremont. Under such circumstances it was a virtue for a Buchanan man to show his colors. There was a solid old Virginian aboard; and his open and intelligent countenance— peculiar, it seems to me, to Virginia— denoted that he was a good-hearted man. I was glad to see him defend his side of politics with so much zeal against the Fremonters. He argued against half a dozen of them with great spirit and sense. In spite of the fervor of his opponents, however, they treated him with proper respect and kindness. It was between eleven and twelve when I arrived at Zanesville. I hastened to the Stacy House with my friend, J. E B. (a young gentleman on his way to Iowa, whose acquaintance I regard it as good luck to have made). The Stacy House could give us lodgings, but not a mouthful of refreshments. As the next best thing, we descended to a restaurant, which seemed to be in a very drowsy condition, where we soon got some oyster and broiled chicken, not however without paying for it an exorbitant price. I rather think, however, I shall go to the Stacy House again when next I visit Zanesville, for, on the whole, I have no fault to find with it. Starting at eight the next morning, we were four hours making the distance (59 miles) from Zanesville to Columbus. The road passes through a country of unsurpassed loveliness. Harvest fields, the most luxuriant, were everywhere in view. At nearly every stopping-place the boys besieged us with delicious apples and grapes, too tempting to be resisted. We had an hour to spend at Columbus, which, after booking our names at the Neil House for dinner— and which is a capital house— we partly spent in a walk about the city. It is the capital of the state, delightfully situated on the Scioto river, and has a population in the neighborhood of 20,000. The new Capitol there is being built on a scale of great magnificence. Though the heat beat down intensely, and the streets were dusty, we were "bent on seeing the town." We— my friend B. and myself— had walked nearly half a mile down one of the fashionable streets for dwellings, when we came to a line which was drawn across the sidewalk in front of a residence, which, from the appearance, might have belonged to one of the upper-ten. The line was in charge of two or three little girls, the eldest of whom was not over twelve. She was a bright-eyed little miss, and had in her face a good share of that metal which the vulgar think is indispensable to young lawyers. We came to a gradual pause at sight of this novel obstruction. "Buchanan, Fillmore, or Fremont?" said she, in a tone of dogmatical interrogatory. B. was a fervid Fremonter— he probably thought she was— so he exclaimed, "Vermont for ever!" I awaited the sequel in silence. "Then you may go round," said the little female politician. "You may go round," and round we went, not a little amused at such an exhibition of enthusiasm. I remember very well the excitement during the campaign of 1840; and I did my share with the New Hampshire boys in getting up decoy cider barrels to humbug the Whigs as they passed in their barouches to attend some great convention or hear Daniel Webster. But it seems to me there is much more political excitement during this campaign than there was in 1840. Flagstaffs and banners abound in the greatest profusion in every village. Every farm-house has some token of its polities spread to the breeze.

At twenty minutes past one— less or more— we left Columbus, and after travelling 158 miles, *via* Dayton, we came to Indianapolis, the great "Railroad City," as it is called, of the west. It was half past nine when we arrived there. I did not have time to go up to the Bates House, where I once had the pleasure of stopping, but concluded to get supper at a hotel near the depot, where there was abundant time to go through the ceremony of eating. It strikes me that Indianapolis would be an agreeable place to reside in. There are some cities a man feels at home in as soon as he gets into them; there are others which make him homesick; just as one will meet faces which in a moment make a good impression on him, or which leave a dubious or disagreeable impression. That city has 16,000 people. Its streets are wide, and its walks convenient. All things denote enterprise, liberality, and comfort. It is 210 miles from Indianapolis to this city, *via* Lafayette and Michigan City. We ought to have made the time in less than twelve hours, and, but for protracted detentions at Lafayette and Michigan City, we would have done so. We reached the latter place at daylight, and there waited about the depot in dull impatience for the Detroit and Chicago train. It is the principal lake harbor in Indiana.

It is about two years since I was last in Chicago; and as I have walked about its streets my casual observation confirms the universal account of its growth and prosperity. I have noticed some new and splendid iron and marble buildings in the course of completion. Chicago is a great place to find old acquaintances. For its busy population comprises citizens from every section of the United States, and from every quarter of the globe. The number of its inhabitants is now estimated at 100,000. Everybody that can move is active. It is a city of activity. Human thoughts are all turned towards wealth.

All seem to he contending in the race for riches: some swift and daring on the open course; some covertly lying low for a by-path. You go along the streets by jerks: down three feet to the street here; then up four slippery steps to the sidewalk there. Here a perfect crowd and commotion— almost a mob— because the drawbridge is up. You would think there was a wonderful celebration coming off at twelve, and that everybody was hurrying through his work to be in season for it. Last year 20,000,000 bushels of grain were brought into Chicago. Five years ago there were not a hundred miles of railroad in the state of Illinois. Now there are more than two thousand. Illinois has all the elements of empire. Long may its great metropolis prosper!

LETTER II.

CHICAGO TO ST. PAUL.

Railroads to the Mississippi— Securing passage on the steamboat— The Lady Franklin— Scenery of the Mississippi— Hastings— Growth of settlements

ST. PAUL, October, 1856.

HOW short a time it is since a railroad to the Mississippi was thought a wonder! And now within the state of Illinois four terminate on its banks. Of course I started on one of these roads from Chicago to get to Dunleith. I think it is called the Galena and Chicago Union Road. A good many people have supposed Galena to be situated on the Mississippi river, and indeed railroad map makers have had it so located as long as it suited their convenience— (for they have a remarkable facility in annihilating distance and in making crooked ways straight)— yet the town is some twelve miles from the great river on a narrow but navigable stream. The extent and importance of Rockford, Galena, and Dunleith cannot fail to make a strong impression on the traveller. They are towns of recent growth, and well illustrate that steam-engine sort of progress peculiar now-a-days in the west. Approaching Galena we leave the region of level prairie and enter a mineral country of naked bluffs or knolls, where are seen extensive operations in the lead mines. The trip from Chicago to Dunleith at the speed used on most other roads would be performed in six hours, but ten hours are usually occupied, for what reason I cannot imagine. However, the train is immense, having on board about six or seven hundred first class passengers, and two-thirds as many of the second class. Travelling in the cars out west is not exactly what it is between Philadelphia and New York, or New York and Boston, in this respect: that in the West more families are found, in the cars, and consequently more babies and carpet bags.

It may not be proper to judge of the health of a community by the appearance of people who are seen standing about a railroad station; yet I have often noticed, when travelling through Illinois, that this class had pale and sickly countenances, showing too clearly the traces of fever and ague.

But I wish to speak about leaving the cars at Dunleith and taking the steamboat for St. Paul. There is a tremendous rush for the boats in order to secure state-rooms. Agents of different boats approach the traveller, informing him all about their line of boats, and depreciating the opposition boats. For instance, an agent, or, if you please, a runner of a boat called Lucy— not Long— made the assertion on the levee with great zeal and perfect impunity that no other boat but the said Lucy would leave for St. Paul within twenty-four hours; when it must have been known to him that another boat on the mail line would start that same evening, as was actually the fact. But the activity of the runners was needless; for each boat had more passengers than it could well accommodate. I myself went aboard the " Lady Franklin," one of the mail boats, and was accommodated with a state-room. But what a scene is witnessed for the first two hours after the passengers begin to come aboard! The cabin is almost filled, and a dense crowd surrounds the clerk's office, just as the ticket office of a theatre is crowded on a benefit night. Of course not more than half can get state-rooms and the rest must sleep on the cabin floor. Over two hundred cabin passengers came up on the Lady Franklin. The beds which are made on the floor are tolerably comfortable, as each boat is supplied with an extra number of single mattresses. The Lady Franklin is an old boat, and this is said to be its last season.[1] Two years ago it was one of the excursion fleet to St. Paul, and was then in its prime. But steamboats are short lived. We had three tables set, and those who couldn't get a seat at the first or second sat at the third. There was a choice you may believe, for such was the havoc made with the provisions at the first table that the second and third were not the most inviting. It was amusing to see gentlemen seat themselves in range of the plates as soon as they were laid, and an hour before the table was ready. But the officers were polite— as is generally the case on steamboats till you get down to the second mate— and in the course of a day or two, when the passengers begin to be acquainted, the time wears away pleasantly. We were nearly four days in making the trip. The line of boats of which the Lady Franklin is one, carries the mail at fifty dollars a trip. During the boating season I believe the fare varies from seven to ten dollars to St. Paul.[2] This season there have been two lines of boats running to Minnesota. All of them have made money fast; and next season many more boats will run. The "Northern Belle" is the best boat this season, and usually makes the trip up in two days. The advertised time is thirty hours.

[1 Three weeks after this trip the Lady Franklin was snagged, and became a total toss.]

[2 The following is a table of distances from Galena to St. Paul:

Dubuque,	24	
Dunleith,	1	25
Potosi Landing,	14	39
Waupaton,	10	49
Buena Vista,	5	54
Cassville,	4	58
Guttenberg,	10	68
Clayton,	12	80

Wyalusing,	5	85
McGregor's,	6	91
Prairie du Chien,	4	95
Red House,	5	100
Johnson's Landing,	2	102
Lafayette,	30	132
Columbus,	2	134
Lansing,	1	135
De Soto,	6	141
Victory,	10	151
Badaxe City,	10	161
Warner's Landing,	6	167
Brownsville,	10	177
La Crosse,	12	189
Dacotah,	12	201
Richmond,	6	207
Monteville,	5	212
Homer,	10	222

Winona,	7	229
Fountain City,	12	241
Mount Vernon,	14	255
Minneiska,	4	259
Alma,	15	274
Wabashaw,	10	284
Nelson's Landing,	3	287
Reed's Landing,	2	289
Foot of Lake Pepin,	2	291
North Pepin,	6	297
Johnstown,	2	299
Lake City,	5	304
Central Point,	2	306
Florence,	3	309
Maiden Rock,	3	312
Westerville,	3	315
Wacouta,	12	327
Red Wing,	6	333

Thing's Landing,	7	340
Diamond bluff,	8	348
Prescott,	13	361
Point Douglass,	1	362
Hastings,	3	365
Grey Cloud,	12	377
Pine Bend,	4	381
Red Rock,	8	389
Kaposia,	3	392
St. Paul,	5	397

]

The scenery on the upper Mississippi is reputed to be beautiful. So it is. Yet all river scenery is generally monotonous. One gets tired of looking at high rocky ridges quite as quickly as at more tame and tranquil scenery. The bluffs on either side of the Mississippi, for most of the way between Dunleith and St. Anthony's Falls, constitute some of the most beautiful river scenery in the world. It is seldom that they rise over two hundred feet from the water level, and their height is quite uniform, so that from a distant point of view their summit resembles a huge fortification. Nor, as a general thing, do they present a bold or rocky front. The rise from the river is gradual. Sometimes they rise to a sharp peak, towards the top of which crops out in half circles heavy ridges of limestone. The ravines which seem to divide them into separate elevations, are more thickly wooded, and appear to have been grooved out by the rolling down of deep waters. The most attractive feature of these bluffs — or miniature mountains, as they might be called — is their smooth grassy surface, thinly covered over with shade trees of various kinds. Whoever has seen a large orchard on a hill side can imagine how the sides of these bluffs look. At this season of the year the variegated foliage of the trees gives them a brilliant appearance. It is quite rare to see a bluff which rises gradually enough to admit of its being a good town site. Hence it is that settlements on the banks of the river will never be very numerous. Nature has here interposed against that civilization which adorns the lower Mississippi. It appears to me that all the available points for town sites on the river are taken up as far as the bluffs extend; and some of these will require a great amount of excavation before they can grow to importance.

But there are several thrifty and pleasant villages in Minnesota, on the river, before reaching St. Paul. The first one of importance is Brownsville, where, for some time, was a United States land office. It is 168 miles above Dunleith. Winona, 58 miles farther up, is a larger town. It is said to contain 5000 population. There is a land office there also. But the town stands on land which, in very high water, will run too much risk of inundation. Passing by several other landings and germs of towns, we come to Wacouta, ninety-eight miles above; which is a successful lumber depot. Six miles further on is Red Wing, a place which delighted me on account of its cheerful location. It is growing quite fast, and is the seat of a large Methodist seminary. But the town of Hastings, thirty-two miles above, eclipses everything but St. Paul. It is finely located on rising ground, and the river is there narrow and deep. The boat stopped here an hour, and I had a good opportunity to look about the place. The town appears to have considerable trade with the back country. Its streets are laid out with regularity; its stores and buildings are spacious, durable, and neat. I heard that over $2000 were asked for several of the building lots. A little way into the interior of the town I saw men at work on a stone church; and approaching the spot, I determined to make some inquiries of a boy who was briskly planing boards. First, I asked how much the church was going to cost? About $3000, he replied.

"Are there any other churches in the place?"

"Yes, up there, where they are building."

"What denomination is that?"

"I don't know," he responded. "I only came into the place yesterday."

I thought he was doing well to begin to build churches so soon after his arrival. And from his countenance, I have no doubt he will do well, and become a useful citizen of the state. Hastings has its democratic press— the Dakota Journal, edited by J. C. Dow, a talented young man from New Hampshire. The population of the town is about two thousand. It is thirty-two miles below St. Paul, on the west side of the river. There is nothing of especial interest between the two places.

The great panorama which time paints is but a species of dissolving views. It is but as yesterday since the present sites of towns and cities on the shores just referred to showed only the rude huts of Indian tribes. To-day, the only vestige left there of the Indian are his burying-grounds. Hereafter the rudeness of pioneer life shall be exchanged for a more genial civilization, and the present, then the past, will be looked back to as trivial by men still yearning for the future.

LETTER III.

CITY OF ST. PAUL.

First settlement of St. Paul— Population— Appearance of the city— Fuller House— Visitors— Roads— Minneapolis— St. Anthony— Suspension Bridge.

FULLER HOUSE, ST. PAUL, October, 1856.

THE circumstance of finding a good spring of water first led to the settlement of Boston. It would not be unreasonable to suppose that a similar advantage induced the first settler of St. Paul to locate here; for I do not suppose its pioneers for a long while dreamed of its becoming a place even of its present importance. And here let me mention that St. Paul is not on the west side of the Mississippi, but on the east. Though it is rather too elevated and rough in its natural state to have been coveted for a farm, it is yet just such a spot as a pioneer would like to plant himself upon, that he might stand in his door and have a broad and beautiful view towards the south and west. And when the speculator came he saw that it was at the head of navigation of what be thought was the Upper Mississippi, but which in reality is only the Middle Mississippi. Then stores were put up, small and rude, and trade began to increase with settlers and hunters of furs. Then came the organization of the territory, and the location of the capital here, so that St. Paul began to thrive still more from the crumbs which fell from the government table, as also by that flood of emigration which nothing except the Rocky Mountains has ever stayed from entering a new territory. And now it has passed its doubtful era. It has passed from its wooden to its brick age. Before men are certain of the success of a town, they erect one story pine shops; but when its success appears certain, they build high blocks of brick or granite stores. So now it is common to see four and five story brick or stone buildings going up in St. Paul.

I believe this city numbers at present about 10,000 population. It is destined to increase for a few years still more rapidly than it has heretofore. But that it will be a second Chicago is what I do not expect. It would certainly seem that the high prices demanded for building lots must retard the progress of the place; but I am told the prices have always been as high in proportion to the business and number of population. $500 and upwards is asked for a decent building lot in remote parts of the town.

I have had an agreeable stroll down upon the bluff, south-east from the city, and near the elegant mansion of Mr. Dayton. The first engraving of St. Paul was made from a view taken at that point. As I stood looking at the city, I recalled the picture in Mr. Bond's work, and contrasted its present with the appearance it had three or four years ago. What a change! Three or four steamers were lying at the levee; steam and smoke were shooting forth from the chimneys of numerous manufactories; a ferry was plying the Mississippi, transporting teams and people; church steeples and domes and great warehouses stood in places which were vacant as if but yesterday; busy streets had been built and peopled; rows of splendid dwellings and villas, adorned with delightful terraces and gardens, had been erected. I went out on Sunday morning too, and the view was none the less pleasant. Business was silent; but the church bells were ringing out their sweet and solemn melody, and the mellow sunlight of autumn glittered on the bright roofs and walls in the city. The whole scene revealed the glorious image of that ever advancing civilization which springs from well rewarded labor and general intelligence.

Like all new and growing places in the west, St. Paul has its whiskey shops, its dusty and dirty streets, its up and down sidewalks, and its never-ceasing whirl of business. Yet it has its churches, well filled; its spacious school-houses; its daily newspapers; and well-adorned mansions. There are many cottages and gardens situated on the most elevated part of the city, north and west, which would not suffer by a comparison with those cheerful and elegant residences so numerous for six to ten miles around Boston. From the parlors of these homes one may look down upon the city and upon the smooth bosom of the river. In the streets, too, you see much evidence of opulence and luxury, in the shape of handsome carriages, which are set out to advantage by a first-rate quality of horses.

One element of the success of this city is the public spirit of its leading business men. They have put their hands deep into their pockets to improve and advance the place. In all their rivalry there is an amicable feeling and boundless liberality. They help him that tries to help himself, and help each other in a way that will help them all together; and such kind of enterprises produces grand results. Why, here is a new hotel (the Fuller House) at which I stop, which is surpassed but by very few hotels in the country. It is a first-class house, built of brick, five stories high, and of much architectural beauty. The building itself cost upwards of $100,000, and its furniture over $30,000. Its proprietor is Mr. Long, who has already had good success in this sort of business. One can well imagine the comfort of finding such a house at the end of a long and tedious journey in a new country.

It is estimated that 28,000 people have visited and left St. Paul during the present season. During July and August the travel diminishes, but as soon as autumn sets in it comes on again in daily floods. It is really a novel and interesting state of things one finds on his arrival at the hotel. There are so many people from so many different places! Then everybody is a stranger to almost everybody, and therefore quite willing to get acquainted with somebody. Everybody wants a bit of information on some point. Everybody is going to some place where he thinks somebody has been or is going, and so a great many new acquaintances are made without ceremony or delay; and old acquaintances are revived. I find people who have come from all sections of the country— from the east and the west, and from the south— not adventurers merely, but men of substance and means, who seek a healthier climate and a pleasant home. Nor can I here omit to mention the meeting of my friend, Col. A. J. Whitney, who is one of the pioneers of Minnesota, and with whom I had two years before travelled over the western prairies. A. H. Marshall, Esq., of Concord, N. H., well known as a popular speaker, is also here on a visit.

But what are the roads leading from St. Paul, and what are the facilities of travel to places beyond? These are questions which I suppose some would like to have answered. There is a road to Stillwater, and a stage, which I believe runs daily. That is the route now often taken to Lake Superior. This morning three men came in on that stage from Superior, who have been a week on the journey. The great highway of the territory extends as far as Crow Wing, 130 miles north of here. It passes St. Anthony and several important towns on the eastern bank of the Mississippi. In a day or two I intend to take a journey as far as Crow Wing, and I can then write with more knowledge on the subject.

A very pretty drive out of St. Paul is by the cave. This is an object worth visiting, and is about two miles out of the city. Three or four miles beyond are the beautiful falls of Minnehaha, or laughing water. The drive also takes in Fort Snelling. St. Anthony is on the east side of the Mississippi; Minneapolis is opposite, on the west side. Both places are now large and populous. The main street of St. Anthony is over a mile in length. One of the finest water powers in the Union is an element of growth to both towns. The lumber which is sawed there is immense. A company is undertaking to remove the obstructions to navigation in the river between St. Paul and St. Anthony. $20,000 were raised for the purpose; one-half by the Steamboat Company, and the other half by the people of St. Anthony. The suspension bridge which connects Minneapolis with St. Anthony is familiar to all. It is a fit type of the enterprise of the people. I forget the exact sum I paid as toll when I walked across the bridge — perhaps it was a dime; at any rate I was struck with the answer given by the young man who took the toll, in reply to my inquiry as I returned, if my coming back wasn't included in the toll paid going over? " No," said he, in a very good-natured way, "we don't know anything about coming back; *it's all go ahead in this country."*

LETTER IV.

THE BAR.

Character of the Minnesota bar — Effect of connecting land business with practice — Courts — Recent legislation of Congress as to the territorial judiciary — The code of practice — Practice in land cases — Chances for lawyers in the West — Charles O'Connor — Requisite qualifications of a lawyer — The power and usefulness of a great lawyer — Talfourd's character of Sir William Follett — Blending law with politics — Services of lawyers in deliberative assemblies

ST. PAUL, October, 1856.

I HAVE not yet been inside of a court of justice, nor seen a case tried, since I have been in the territory. But it has been my pleasure to meet one of the judges of the supreme court and several prominent members of the bar. My impression is, that in point of skill and professional ability the Minnesota bar is a little above the average of territorial bars. Here, as in the West generally, the practice is common for lawyers to mix with their profession considerable miscellaneous business, such as the buying and selling of land. The law is too jealous a mistress to permit any divided love, and therefore it cannot be expected that really good lawyers will be found in the ranks of general business agents and speculators. In other words, a broker's office is not a lawyer's office. There are some lawyers here who have attended strictly to the profession, who are ornaments of it, and who have met with good success. The idea has been common, and as fatal as common, that success in legal practice could be easily attained in the West with a small amount of skill and learning. It is true that a poor lawyer aided by some good qualities will sometimes rise to affluence and eminence, though such cases are exceptions. There are able layers in the West, and, though practice may be less formal and subtle than in older communities, ability and skill find their relative advancement and reward, while ignorance and incapacity have their downward tendency just as they do everywhere else. The fees for professional services are liberal, being higher than in the East. Before an attorney can be admitted to practise he must have an examination by, or under the direction of, one of the judges of the supreme court. The provisions of the territorial statutes are quite strict in their tendency to maintain upright practice.

An act of the present congress has created a revolution in the courts of the territory. The organic act, SS 9, provided that the territory should be divided into three judicial districts; "and a district court shall be held in each of said districts by one of the justices of the supreme court, at such times and places *as may be prescribed by law.*" This meant, I suppose, at such times and places as the territorial legislature should prescribe. Accordingly, as population increased and extended, and as counties were established, the territorial legislature increased the places in each district for holding the district court. Either on account of the expense or for some other cause congress has just stepped aside from the doctrine of non-intervention (ch. 124, sec. 5), and abrogated the territorial legislation so far as to provide that there shall be but one place in each of the three districts for holding a district court. The act applies to all territories. In a territory of five or six hundred miles in extent it is of course inconvenient to have but three places for holding courts. The Minnesotians complain that it is an interference with popular sovereignty. It is possible the legislature might have gone to an extreme in creating places for holding courts; and I suppose the judges were kept on the march a good deal of the time. It also looks as if the remedy by congress was extreme. The people say it is a coercive measure to drive them into a state organization.

The administration of justice is secured by a system which is now common to all the territories, with the exception of Kansas. The supreme court consists of the three district judges in full bench.

They hold nisi prius terms in their respective districts, which are called district courts. The judges have a salary of $2000 each, and are appointed for a term of four years, subject to removal by the President. The district courts have chancery jurisdiction in matters where there is not a plain, adequate, and complete remedy at law. (Stat. of Min. ch. 94, sec. 1.) There are also probate courts. Each county has two justices of the peace, who are elected by the people. And I cannot but remark how much better the practice is to elect or appoint a few justices of the peace rather than to allow the office to be degraded by wholesale appointments, as a matter of compliment, according to the usage too common in some Eastern States. The justices of the peace have jurisdiction in civil cases where the amount in question does not exceed $100; and when the amount at issue is over $20 either party may demand a jury of six men to try the case. But there would be little demand for juries if all magistrates were as competent as our enlightened friend Judge Russell.

Special pleading never flourished much in the West. It was never "a favorite with the court" out this way; while the regard which the lawyers have cherished for it has been "distant and respectful." It has been laid on the shelf about as effectually as bleeding in the practice of medicine. The science of special pleading, as it is known in these days— and that in some of the older states— exists in a mitigated form from what it did in the days of Coke and Hale. The opportunities to amend, and the various barriers against admitting a multiplicity of pleas, have rendered the system so much more rational than it once was, that it is doubtful if some of the old English worthies could now identify it. Once a defendant could plead to an action of assumpsit just as many defences as he chose; first, he could deny the whole by pleading the general issue; then he could plead the statute of limitations, infancy, accord and satisfaction, and a dozen other pleas, by which the plaintiff would be deprived of any clue to the real defence. I suppose it was this practice of formal lying which has given rise to the popular error that a lawyer is in the habit of lying, or is obliged to lie, in his arguments. Many people do not know the difference between *pleading*— which is a process in writing to bring the parties to an issue— and the oral arguments of counsel in courts. It is ridiculous to suppose that it is easy or profitable for lawyers to make false statements in their arguments. The opposing counsel is ready to catch at anything of the kind; and if he misstates the evidence, the jury are aware of it; while if he states what is not law, the court generally knows it. So there is no opportunity for lying even if a lawyer should be so disposed. The practice in civil actions as provided by the statutes of Minnesota is similar — if not actually the same — to the New York code of practice. There is but one form of action, called an action of contract. The only pleading on the part of the plaintiff is, 1st, the complaint; 2d, the reply. On the part of the defendant, 1st, demurrer; or 2d, the answer. (Stats. ch. 70, sec. 58.) The complaint must contain, 1st, the title of the cause, specifying the name of the court in which the action is brought and the names of the parties to the action, plaintiff and defendant; 2d, a statement of the facts constituting the cause of action in ordinary and concise language, without repetition, and in such a manner as to enable a person of common understanding to know what is intended; 3d, a demand of the relief to which the plaintiff supposes himself entitled. If the recovery of money be demanded the amount must be stated. (Ibid. sec. 59.)

While testifying my approval of this code of practice as a whole, I cannot resist saying that in many respects it is not so systematic as the Massachusetts code, which was devised by Messrs. Curtis (now Mr. Justice), Lord, and Chapman. That code is one of the best in the world. And if I may be allowed one word more about special pleading, I would say that there is no branch of law which will better reward study. Without mentioning the practice in the U. S. courts, which requires, certainly, a knowledge of special pleading, no one can read the old English reports and text books with much profit, who is ignorant of the principles of that science.

A class of business peculiar to new territories and states arises from the land laws. A great many pre-emption cases are contested before the land officers, in which the services of lawyers are required. This fact will partly explain why there are, generally, so many lawyers located in the vicinity of a land office. In a community that is newly settled the title to property must often be in dispute; and however much averse people may be to going to law, they find it frequently indispensable, if they wish to have their rights settled on a firm basis.

The opinion prevails almost universally in the East that a lawyer can do best in the West. In some respects he can. If he cannot do a good deal better, he is not compensated for going. I had the pleasure of a conversation last summer with one of the most eminent members of the New York bar (Mr. O'Connor), on this very subject. It was his opinion that western lawyers begin sooner to enjoy their reputation than the lawyers in the eastern cities. This is true; and results from there being less competition in newer communities. "A lawyer among us," said Mr. O'Connor, "seldom acquires eminence till he begins to turn gray." Nevertheless, there is no field so great and so certain in the long run, in which one may become really a great lawyer, as in some of our large commercial cities, whether of the East or the West. To admit of the highest professional eminence there must be a large and varied business; and a lawyer must devote himself almost exclusively to law. And then, when this great reputation is acquired, what does it amount to? Something now, but not much hereafter. The great lawyer lives a life of toil and excitement. Often does it seem to "break on the fragments of a reviving dream." His nerves are worn by the troubles of others; for the exercise of the profession, as has been said by a brilliant lawyer, "involves intimate participation with the interests, hopes, fears, passions, affections, and vicissitudes of many lives." And yet merely as a lawyer, he seldom leaves any durable vestige of his fame behind him — hardly a fortune. But if his fame is transient and mortal, there is some equivalent in the pleasure of triumph and the consciousness of power. There is no man so powerful as the great lawyer. The wealth and the character of his fellow men often depend upon him. His clients are sometimes powerful corporations, or cities, or states. Crowded courts listen to his eloquence year after year; and no one has greater freedom of speech than he. The orator and politician may be wafted into a conspicuous place for a brief period, and fall again when popular favor has cooled; yet the lawyer is rising still higher, nor can the rise and fall of parties shake him from his high pedestal; for the tenure of his power is not limited. He is, too, one of the most serviceable protectors of the liberties of his country. It was as a lawyer that Otis thundered against writs of assistance. The fearless zeal of Somers, in defence of the seven bishops, fanned the torch of liberty at the beginning of the great English revolution.

Erskine and Brougham did more as lawyers to promote freedom of the press, than as Statesmen.

I cannot refrain from inserting here Mr. Justice Talfourd's interesting analysis of the professional abilities of Follett: "It may be well, while the materials for investigation remain, to inquire into the causes of success, so brilliant and so fairly attained by powers which have left so little traces of their progress. Erskine was never more decidedly at the head of the common law bar than Follett; compared with Follett he was insignificant in the house of commons; his career was chequered by vanities and weaknesses from which that of Follett was free; and yet even if he had not been associated with the greatest constitutional questions of his time and their triumphant solution, his fame would live by the mere force and beauty of his forensic eloquence as long as our language. But no collection of the speeches of Follett has been made; none will ever be attempted; no speech he delivered is read, except perchance as part of an interesting trial, and essential to its story, and then the language is felt to be poor, the cadences without music, and the composition vapid and spiritless; although, if studied with a view to the secrets of forensic success, with a 'learned spirit of human dealing,' in connexion with the facts developed and the difficulties encountered, will supply abundant materials for admiration of that unerring skill which induced the repetition of fortunate topics, the dexterous suppression of the most stubborn things when capable of oblivion, and the light evasive touch with which the speaker fulfilled his promise of not forgetting others which could not be passed over, but which, if deeply considered, might he fatal. If, however, there was no principle of duration in his forensic achievements, there can be doubt of the esteem in which they were held or the eagerness with which they were sought. His supremacy in the minds of clients was more like the rage of a passion for a youthful Roscius or an extraordinary preacher, than the result of deliberate consideration; and yet it prevailed, in questions not of an evening's amusement, but of penury or riches, honor or shame. Suitors were content, not only to make large sacrifices for the assured advantage of his advocacy, but for the bare chance— the distant hope— of having some little part (like that which Phormio desires to retain in Thais) of his faculties, with the certainty of preventing their opposition. There was no just ground, in his case, for the complaint that he received large fees for services he did not render; for the chances were understood by those who adventured in his lottery; in which after all there were comparatively few blanks. His *name* was 'a tower of strength,' which it was delightful to know that the adverse faction wanted, and which inspired confidence even on the back of the brief of his forsaken junior, who bore the burden and heat of the day for a fifth of the fee which secured that name. Will posterity ask what were the powers thus sought, thus prized, thus rewarded, and thus transient? They will be truly told that he was endowed, in a remarkable degree, with some moral qualities which smoothed his course and charmed away opposition, and with some physical advantages which happily set off his intellectual gifts; that he was blessed with a temper at once gentle and even; with a gracious manner and a social temperament; that he was without jealousy of the solid or showy talents of others, and willingly gave them the amplest meed of praise; that he spoke with all the grace of modesty, yet with the assurance of perfect mastery over his subject, his powers, and his audience; and yet they will scarcely recognise in these excellencies sufficient reasons for his extraordinary success. To me, the true secret of his peculiar strength appeared to lie in the possession of two powers which rarely co-exist in the same mind— extraordinary subtlety of perception and as remarkable simplicity of execution. In the first of these faculties— in the intuitive power of common sense, which is the finest essence of experience, whereby it attains 'to something of prophetic strain'— he excelled all his contemporaries except Lord Abinger, with whom it was more liable to be swayed by prejudice or modified by taste, as it was adorned with happier graces. The perfection of this faculty was remarkably exemplified in the fleeting visits he often paid to the trials of causes which he had left to the conduct of his juniors; a few words, sometimes a glance, sufficed to convey to his mind the exact position of complicated affairs, and enabled him to decide what should be done or avoided; and where the interference of any other moral advocate would have been dangerous, he often rendered good service, and, which was more extraordinary, never did harm. So his unrivalled aptitude for legal reasoning, enabled him to deal with authorities as he dealt with facts; if unprepared for an argument, he could find its links in the chaos of an index, and make an imposing show of learn-

ing out of a page of Harrison; and with the aid of the interruptions
of the bench, which he could as dexterously provoke as parry, could
find the right clue and conduct a luminous train of reasoning to a
triumphant close. His most elaborate arguments, though not com-
parable in essence with those of his chief opponent, Lord Camp-
bell— which, in comprehensive outline, exact logic, felicitous illustration, and harmonious structure, excelled all others I have heard—
were delivered in tones so nicely adapted to the minds and ears of
the judges, with an earnestness so winning, and a confidence so
contagious, that they made a judgment on his side not only a necessity, but a pleasure.

"The other faculty, to which, in combination with his subtlety of
understanding, the excellence of his advocacy may be attributed, is
one more rarely possessed— and scarcely ever in such association—
the entire singleness of a mind equally present in every part of a
cause. If the promotion of the interest of the client were an advocate's highest duty, it would be another name for the exactest virtue;
and inasmuch as that interest is not, like the objects of zeal, fixed in
character, but liable to frequent change, the faculty of directing the
whole power of the understanding to each shifting aspect of the
cause in its minutest shadowings without the guidance of an inflex-
ible law, is far more wonderful, if far less noble, than a singleness of
devotion to right. It has an integrity of its own, which bears some
affinity to that honesty which Baillie Nichol Jarvie attributes to his
Highland kinsman. Such honesty— that is, the entire devotion of all
the faculties to the object for which it was retained, without the
lapse of a moment's vanity or indolence, with unlimited vision and
unceasing activity— was Follett's beyond all other advocates of our
time. To the presentment of truth, or sophism, as the cause might
require, he gave his entire mind with as perfect oblivion of self as
the most heroic sufferer for principle. The faculty which in Glad-
stone, the statesman, applied to realities and inspired only by the
desire to discover the truth and to clothe it in language, assumes, in
the minds of superficial observers, the air of casuistry from the nice-
ty of its distinctions and the earnest desire of the speaker to present
truth in its finest shades— in Follett, the advocate, applied indis-
criminately to the development of the specious shows of things as of
their essences, wore all the semblance of sincerity; and, in one sense,

deserved it. No fears, no doubts, no scruples shook him. Of the license which advocacy draws from sympathy with the feelings of those it represents, he made full use, with unhesitating power; for his reason, of 'large discourse,' was as pliable as the affections of the most sensitive nature. Nor was he diverted from his aim by any figure or fancy: if he neither exalted his subject by imagination, nor illustrated it by wit, nor softened its details by pathos, he never made it the subject of vain attempts at the exhibition of either. He went into the arena, stripped of all encumbrance, to win, and contended studious only and always of victory. His *presence of mind* was not merely the absence of external distraction, nor the capacity of calling up all energies on an emergency, but the continued application of them equally to the duty of each moment. There are few speakers, even of fervid sincerity and zeal, whose thoughts do not frequently run before or beside the moment's purpose; whose wits do not sometimes wander on to some other part of the case than that they are instantly discussing; who do not anticipate some future effect, or dally with some apprehension of future peril, while they should consider only the next word or sentence. This momentary desertion of the exact purpose never occurred to Follett; he fitted the thought to its place; the word to the thought; and allowed the action only to take care of itself, as it always will with an earnest speaker. His, therefore, was rather the artlessness than the art of advocacy — its second nature — justly appreciated by those to whose interests it was devoted; but not fully understood even by the spectator of its exertion; dying with the causes in which it was engaged, and leaving no vestiges except in their success. Hence the blank which is substituted for the space he filled in human affairs. The modest assurance, the happy boldness, the extemporaneous logic, all that 'led but to the grave,' exist, like the images of departed actors, only in the recollection of those who witnessed them, till memory shall fade into tradition, and tradition dwindle down to a name." (Supplement to Vacation Rambles, p. 115.) The eagerness with which the talents of Sir William Follett were sought, forcibly illustrates the truth of a remark, made to me in the course of some friendly advice, by one who may be ranked among the most brilliant advocates who have adorned the American Bar (now in the highest office in the nation), that to attain the highest rank in the legal profession, a lawyer must have such abilities and character as will "compel" patronage.

He, however, who enters the profession here or elsewhere merely as a stepping stone to political preferment, need not expect great success, even though he may acquire some temporary advancement. The day is past when lawyers could monopolize every high place in the state. The habit of public speaking is not now confined to the learned professions. Our peculiar system of education has trained up a legion of orators and politicians outside of the bar. Now-a-days a man must have other qualifications besides the faculty of speech-making to win the prize in politics. He must be a man of comprehensive ability, and thoroughly identified with the interests of the people, before he can secure much popular favor, or else he must be possessed of such shining talents and character that his fellow men will take a pride in advancing him to conspicuous and responsible trusts. Let a man have a part or all of these qualifications, however, and with them the experience and tact of a lawyer, and he will of course make a more valuable public servant, especially if he is placed in a deliberative body. The British cabinets have always relied vastly on the support afforded them in the house of commons by their attorneys and solicitors general, whether it consisted in the severe and solemn logic of Romilly, in the cool and ready arguments of Scarlett, or the acute and irresistible oratory of Sir William Follett. The education of a lawyer;— his experience as a manager; his art of covering up weak points, his ready and adroit style of speaking;— all serve to make him peculiarly valuable to his own party, and dangerous to an opposition in a deliberative body. But the fact that a man is a lawyer does not advance him in politics so much as it once did. Fortunate it is so! For though learning will always have its advantages, yet no profession ought to have exclusive privileges. Nor need the lawyer repine that it is so, inasmuch as it is for his benefit, if he desires success in the profession, to discard the career of politics. The race is not to the swift, and he can afford to wait for the legitimate honors of the bar. I will conclude by saying that I regard Minnesota as a good field for an upright, industrious, and competent lawyer. For those of an opposite class, I have never yet heard of a very promising field.

LETTER V.

ST. PAUL TO CROW WING IN TWO DAYS.

Stages— Roads— Rum River— Indian treaty— Itasca— Sauk Rapids— Watab at midnight— Lodging under difficulties,— Little Rock River— Character of Minnesota streams— Dinner at Swan River— Little Falls— Fort Ripley— Arrival at Crow Wing.

CROW WING, October, 1856.

HERE I am, after two days drive in a stage, at the town of Crow Wing, one hundred and thirty miles, a little west of north, from St. Paul. I will defer, however, any remarks on Crow Wing, or the many objects of interest hereabout, till I have mentioned a few things which I saw coming up. Between St. Paul and this place is a tri-weekly line of stages. The coaches are of Concord manufacture, spacious and comfortable; and the entire equipage is well adapted to the convenience of travellers. Next season, the enterprising proprietors, Messrs. Chase and Allen, who carry the mail, intend establishing a daily line. I left the Fuller House in the stage at about five in the morning. There was only a convenient number of passengers till we arrived at St. Anthony, where we breakfasted; but then our load was more than doubled, and we drove out with nine inside and about seven outside, with any quantity of baggage. The road is very level and smooth; and with the exception of encountering a few small stamps where the track has been diverted for some temporary impediment, and also excepting a few places where it is exceedingly sandy, it is an uncommonly superior road. It is on the eastern bank of the Mississippi, and was laid out very straight. But let me remark that everybody who travels it seems conscious that it is a government road. There are several bridges, and they are often driven over at a rapid rate, much to their damage. When Minnesota shall have a state government, and her towns or counties become liable for the condition of the roads, people will doubtless be more economical of the bridges, even though the traveller be not admonished to walk his horse, or to "keep to the right," &c.

Emerging from St. Anthony, the undulating aspect of the country ceases, and we enter upon an almost unbroken plain. A leading characteristic of the scenery is the thin forests of oak, commonly called oak openings. The soil appears to be rich.

Seven miles from St. Anthony is a tidy settlement called Manomin, near the mouth of Rice river. But the first place of importance which we reached is Anoka, a large and handsome village situated on Rum river. It is twenty-five miles from St. Paul. The river is a large and beautiful stream and affords good water-power, in the development of which Anoka appears to thrive. A vast number of pine logs are annually floated down the river and sawed into lumber at the Anoka mills. The settlers are principally from Maine. By the treaty of 22d February, 1855, with three bands of the Chippewa Indians, an appropriation of $5000 was set apart for the construction of a road from the mouth of Rum river to Mille Lac. The road is half completed.

We took an early dinner at Itasca, having come thirty-two miles. Itasca is quite an unassuming place, and not so pretty as its name. But I shall always cherish a good-will for the spot, inasmuch as I got a first-rate dinner there. It was all put upon the table before we sat down, so that each one could help himself; and as it consisted of very palatable edibles, each one did help himself quite liberally. We started on soon afterwards, with a new driver and the third set of horses; but with the disagreeable consciousness that we had still before us the largest part of the day's journey. In about three hours we came to Big Lake, or, as it is sometimes called, Humboldt. The lake is anything but a big lake, being the size of a common New England pond. But then all such sheets of water are called lakes in this part of the country. It is a clear body of water, abounding with fine fish, and has a beautiful shore of pebbles. Several similar sheets of water are passed on the journey, the shores of which present a naked appearance. There is neither the trace of a stream leading from or to them, nor, with few exceptions, even a swamp in their vicinity.

Sauk Rapids is 44 miles from Itasca, and it was late when we reached there. But, late as it was, we found a large collection of people at the post office waiting for the mail. They appeared to have had a caucus, and were discussing politics with much animation. There is at Sauk Rapids a local land office. That is of more advantage to a place than being the county seat. In a short time, however, some of the land offices will be removed further west for the convenience of settlers. The village is finely situated on rising ground, and contains some handsome residences.

It was midnight when we arrived at Watab, where we were to lodge. The weather had been delightful during the day, but after nightfall a high wind rose and filled the air with dust. I descended from the stage— for I had rode upon the outside— with self-satisfied emotions of having come eighty-two miles since morning. The stage-house was crowded. It is a two-story building, the rooms of which are small. I went to bed, I was about to say, without any supper. But that was not so. I didn't get any supper, it is true, neither did I get a bed; for they were all occupied. The spare room on the floor was also taken. The proprietor, however, was accommodating, and gave me a sort of a lounge in rather a small room where three or four other men, and a dog, were sleeping on the floor. I fixed the door ajar for ventilation, and with my overcoat snugly buttoned around me, though it was not cold, addressed myself to sleep. In the morning I found that one of the occupants was an ex-alderman from the fifth ward of New York; and that in the room over me slept no less a personage than Parker H. French. I say I ascertained these facts in the morning. Mr. French came to Watab a few weeks ago with a company of mechanics, and has been rushing the place ahead with great zeal. He appears to make a good impression on the people of the town.

A heavy rain had fallen during the night; the stage was but moderately loaded, and I started out from Watab, after breakfast the next morning, in bright spirits. Still the road is level, and at a slow trot the team makes better time than a casual observer is conscious of. Soon we came to Little Rock River, which is one of the crookedest streams that was ever known of. We are obliged to cross it twice within a short space. Twelve miles this side we cross the beautiful Platte River. It would make this letter much more monotonous than it is, I fear, were I to name all the rivers we pass. They are very numerous: and as they increase the delight of the traveller, so are they also a delight and a convenience to the settler. Like the rivers of

New England, they are clear and rapid, and furnish abundant means for water-power. The view which we catch of the Mississippi is frequent, but brief, as the road crosses its curves in the most direct manner. Much of the best land on either side of the road is in the hands of speculators, who purchased it at public sale, or afterwards plastered it over with land warrants. There is evidence of this on the entire route; for, although we pass populous villages, and a great many splendid farms, the greater part of the land is still unoccupied. The soil is dark colored, but in some places quite mealy; everywhere free from stones, and susceptible of easy cultivation.

We arrived at Swan River at about one o'clock, where we dined on wild ducks. That is a village also of considerable importance; but it is not so large as Little Falls, which is three miles this side. At that place the Mississippi furnishes a good water power. It has a spacious and tidy hotel, several stores, mechanics' shops, a saw-mill, &c. At Belle Prairie we begin to see something of the Chippewas. The half-breeds have there some good farms, and the school-house and the church denote the progress of civilization. It was near sunset when we reached Fort Ripley. The garrison stands on the west bank of the Mississippi, but the reservation extends several miles on both sides. The stage crosses the river on the ferry to leave the mail and then returns. The great flag was still flying from the high staff, and had an inspiring influence. Like most of our inland military posts, Port Ripley has no stone fortifications. It is neatly laid out in a square, and surrounded by a high protective fence. Three or four field-pieces stand upon the bank of the river fronting it, and at some distance present a warlike attitude. The rest of the trip, being about five miles, was over the reservation, on which, till we come to Crow Wing, are no settlements. Here I gladly alighted from the coach, and found most comfortable and agreeable entertainment at a house which stands on the immediate bank of the river.

LETTER VI.

THE TOWN OF CROW WING.

Scenery— First settlement of Crow Wing— Red Lake Indians— Mr. Morrison— Prospects of the town— Upper navigation— Mr. Beaulieu— Washington's theory as to Norfolk— Observations on the growth of towns.

CROW WING, October, 1856.

I AM highly gratified with the appearance of this place. Mr. Burke says— " In order that we should love our country, our country should first be lovely," and there is much wisdom in the remark. Nature has done so much for this locality that one could be contented to live here on quite a moderate income. The land is somewhat elevated, near the bank of the Mississippi, affording a pleasant view over upon the western side, both above and below the two graceful mouths of the Crow Wing River. Towards the east and north, after a few miles, the view is intercepted by a higher ridge of land covered with timber; or, by the banks of the Mississippi itself, as from this point we begin to ascend it in a northeasterly course.

Crow Wing was selected as a trading post upwards of twenty years ago. Mr. McDonnald, who still resides here, was, I believe, the first white settler. Till within a recent period it was the headquarters of the Mississippi tribe of Chippewas, and the principal trading depot with the Chippewas generally. Here they brought their furs, the fruits of their buffalo and their winter hunts, and their handicraft of beads and baskets, to exchange for clothing and for food. Thus the place was located and settled on long before there was a prospect of its becoming a populous town. Mr. Rice, the delegate in congress, if I mistake not, once had a branch store here with several men in his employ. The principal traders at present are Mr. Abbee and Mr. Beaulieu, who have large and well selected stocks of goods. The present population of white persons probably numbers a hundred souls. The place now has a more populous appearance on account of the presence of a caravan of Red Lake Indians, who have come down about four hundred miles to trade. They are encamped round about in tents or birch bark lodges, as it may happen to be. In passing some of them, I saw the squaws busily at work on the grass outside of the lodge in manufacturing flag carpets. The former Indian residents are now removed to their reservation in the fork of the

Mississippi and Crow Wing rivers, where their agency is now established.

The houses here are very respectable in size, and furnished in metropolitan style and elegance. The farms are highly productive, and the grazing for stock unequalled. There is a good ferry at the upper end of the town, at a point where the river is quite narrow and deep. You can be taken over with a horse for twenty-five cents; with a carriage, I suppose, the tariff is higher.

Perhaps one cause of my favorable impression of Crow Wing is the excellent and home-like hotel accommodations which I have found. The proprietor hardly assumes to keep a public-house, and yet provides his guests with very good entertainment; and I cannot refrain from saying that there is no public-house this side of St. Paul where the traveller will be better treated. Mr. Morrison— for that is the proprietor's name— came here fifteen years ago, having first come into this region in the service of John Jacob Astor. He married one of the handsomest of the Chippewa maidens, who is now his faithful wife and housekeeper, and the mother of several interesting and amiable children. Mr. M. is the postmaster. He has been a member of the territorial legislature, and his name has been given to a large and beautiful county. I judge that society has been congenial in the town. The little church, standing on an eminence, indicates some union of sentiment at least, and a regard for the higher objects of life. Spring and summer and autumn must be delightful seasons here, and bring with them the sweetest tranquillity. Nor are the people shut out from the world in winter; for then there is travel and intercourse and traffic. So are there pleasures and recreation peculiar to the season.

But the serene and quiet age of the settlement is near its close. Enterprise and speculation, with their bustle and turmoil, have laid hold of it. The clank of the hammer, the whistle of steamboats, the rattling of carts, heaps of lumber and of bricks, excavations and gratings, short corners and rough unshapen walks, will usurp the quiet and the regularity of the place. Indeed a man ought to make a fortune to compensate for residing in a town during the first years of its rapid building. The streets appear, on the map, to be well laid out. A number of purchasers of lots are preparing to build; and a few new buildings are already going up. As near as I am able to learn, the things which conduce to its availability as a business place are these— First, it is the beginning of the Upper Mississippi navigation. From this point steamboats can go from two to three hundred miles. But they cannot pass below, on account of the obstructions near Fort Ripley, at Little Falls, and at Sauk Rapids. This of course is a great element in its future success, as the country above in the valley of the river is destined to be thickly settled, and boats will run between this point and the settlements along the river. It will also be a large lumber market, for the pine forests begin here and extend along the river banks for hundreds of miles, while the facility of getting the logs down is unexceptionable. The territory north of Crow Wing is now open for settlers to a great distance, the Indian title having been extinguished. Two land districts have also been established, which will be an inducement for fresh emigration. There is no other place but this to supply these settlements; at least none so convenient. A great deal of timber will also come down the Crow Wing River, which is a large stream, navigable three months in the year. Arrangements are complete for building a steamboat the ensuing winter, at this very place, to begin running in the spring as far up as Ojibeway. Next season there will be a daily line of stages between this and St. Paul. I understand also that it is intended next summer to connect Crow Wing with the flourishing town of Superior by stage. It will require considerable energy to do this thing; but if it can be done, it will be a great blessing to the traveller as well as a profit to the town. The journey from St. Paul to Lake Superior via Crow Wing can then be performed in three days, while on the usual route it now occupies a week. Such are some of the favorable circumstances which corroborate the expectation of the growth of this place. The southern or lower portion of the town is included within the Fort Ripley reserve, and though several residences are situated on it, no other buildings can be put up without a license from the commanding officer; nor can any lots be sold from that portion until the reserve is cut down. With the upper part of the town it is different. Mr. C. H. Beaulieu, long a resident of the place, is the proprietor of that part, and has already, I am informed, made some extensive sales of lots. He is one of those lucky individuals, who have sagacity to locate on an available spot, and patience to wait the opening of a splendid fortune.[1]

[1 Since this letter was written, Mr. Thomas Cathcart has purchased a valuable claim opposite Crow Wing at the mouth of the river, which I should think was an available town site.]

My observation and experience in regard to town sites have taught me an important fact: that as much depends on the public spirit, unity of action, and zeal of the early proprietors, as upon the locality itself. The one is useless without these helps. General Washington wrote an able essay to prove the availability of Norfolk, Va., as the great commercial metropolis of the country. He speculated upon its being the great market for the West. His imagination pictured out some such place as New York now is, as its future. The unequalled harbor of Norfolk, and the resources of the country all around it, extending as far, almost, as thought could reach, might well have encouraged the theory of Washington. But munificence and energy and labor have built up many cities since then, which had not half the natural advantages of Norfolk, while Norfolk is far behind. A little lack of enterprise, a little lack of harmony and liberality, may, in the early days of a town, divert business and improvements from a good location, till in a short time an unheard-of and inferior place totally eclipses it. Knowing this to be the case, I have been careful in my previous letters not to give too much importance to many of the town sites which have been commended to me along my journey. I do not discover any of these retarding circumstances about Crow Wing. I must conclude at this paragraph, however, in order to take a horseback ride to the Chippewa agency. In my next I intend to say something about the Indians, pine timber, and the country above here in general.

LETTER VII.

CHIPPEWA INDIANS. — HOLE-IN-THE-DAY.

Description of the Chippewa tribes— Their habits and customs— Mission at Gull Late— Progress in farming— Visit to Hole-in-the-day— His enlightened character— Reflections on Indian character, and the practicability of their civilization— Their education— Mr. Manypenny's exertions.

CROW WING, October, 1856.

I CONSIDER myself exceedingly fortunate in having had a good opportunity for observing the condition of the Chippewa Indians. Sometime ago I saw enough of the Indians in another part of the country to gratify my curiosity as to their appearance and habits; and as I have always felt a peculiar interest in their destiny, my present observations have been with a view to derive information as to the best means for their improvement. The whole number of Chippewas in Minnesota is not much over 2200. They are divided into several bands, each band being located a considerable distance from the other. The Mississippi band live on their reservation, which begins a few miles above here across the river, while the Pillagor and Lake Winnibigoshish bands are some three hundred miles further north. The agency of the Chippewas is on the reservation referred to, a little north of the Crow Wing River, and six miles distant from this town. To come down more to particulars, however, and adopt words which people here would use, I might say that the agency is on Gull River, a very clear and pretty stream, which flows from a lake of that name, into the Crow Wing. I passed the agency yesterday, and two miles beyond, in order to visit Pug-o-na-ke-shick, or Hole-in-the-day, the principal and hereditary chief of the Chippewas. Mr. Herriman, the agent, resides at the agency, in compliance with the regulation of the Indian bureau, which requires agents to reside among the Indians. I strongly suspect there are many people who would think it unsafe to travel alone among the Chippewas. But people who live about here would ridicule the idea of being afraid of violence or the slightest molestation from them, unless indeed the fellows were intoxicated. For my part, a walk on Boston common on a summer morning could not seem more quiet and safe than a ramble on horseback among the homes of these Indians. I spoke to a good many. Though naturally reserved and silent, they return a friendly salutation with a pleasant smile.

Their old costume is still retained as a general thing. The blanket is still worn instead of coats. Sometimes the men wear leggins, but often go with their legs naked. A band is generally worn upon the head with some ornament upon it. A feather of the war eagle worn in the head-band of a brave, denotes that he has taken the scalp of an enemy or performed some rare feat of daring. An Indian does not consider himself in full dress without his war hatchet or weapons. I meet many with long-stemmed pipes, which are also regarded as an ornamental part of dress. They appear pleased to have anything worn about them attract attention. They are of good size, taller than the Winnebagoes, and of much lighter complexion than tribes living five hundred miles further south. Herein the philosopher on the cooking of men is confirmed. Their hair is black, long, and straight; and some are really good-looking. There are but few who still paint. Those in mourning paint their faces black. What I have seen of their houses raises high hopes of their advancement in civilization. We can now begin to lay aside the word lodge and say house. Over a year ago, Mr. Herriman promised every one a good cooking stove who would build himself a comfortable house. This promise had a good effect, for several houses were built. But the want of windows and several other conveniences, which are proper fixtures, gives their dwellings a desolate appearance to one who looks to a higher standard of comfort. Of course I saw a few of the men at the store (for there is a store at the agency), spending their time, as too many white men do in country villages. Eight miles beyond the agency, on Gull Lake, is a mission. It has been under the charge of Rev. J. L. Breck, a gentleman of high culture, and whose enlightened and humane exertions in behalf of the Indians have received much commendation both from the agent and Gov. Gorman, the Superintendent. He has been at the mission four years. While he had the benefit of the school-fund, he had in his school, under his own roof, 35 pupils; since that was withheld, the number of pupils has been 22. Mr. Breck will soon remove to Leech Lake, and will be succeeded by a gentleman who comes well recommended from a theological institution in Wisconsin. I desired very much to go as far as the mission, but from Crow Wing and back it would have been thirty miles, and it was otherwise inconvenient on account of the rain. The Indians are beginning to farm a little. They begin with gardens. Their support is chiefly from the annuities paid by the United States, which are principally received in some sort of dry goods. The goods are furnished by contract, and the price paid for them is about enough, if all stories are true. They also derive some support from their fur hunts and by fishing. Buffaloes are still hunted successfully beyond the Red River of the North. They bring home the furs, and also the best parts of the meat. The meat is preserved by being partially cooked in buffalo fat, cut into small pieces, and sewed up very tight in the hide of the animal. It is called *pemmican,* and sells here for twenty-five cents a pound. It is broken to pieces like pork scraps, and the Indians regard it as a great luxury.

From the agency I hastened on to see Hole-in-the-day (Pug-o-na-ke-shick, his Indian name, means, literally, *Hole-in-the-sky).* He is a famous chief, having in his youth distinguished himself for bold exploits and severe endurance. But what most entitles him to attention is the very exemplary course he has pursued in attempting to carry out the wishes of the government in bringing his race to the habits of civilized life. It was principally through his influence that a treaty was made between his tribe and the United States, and after it went into effect he turned his attention to farming. Previous to the treaty he was supported as chief by the tribal revenue. He has succeeded well. Over a year ago the receipts of what he sold from his farm, aside from what his household needed, amounted to over two hundred dollars. At length, after riding a mile and a half without passing a habitation, over a fertile prairie, I came in sight of his house. He lives near a small lake, and north of him is a large belt of heavy pine timber. He has an excellent farm, well fenced and well cultivated. His house is in cottage style, and of considerable length; spacious, neat, and well furnished. Arriving at the door I dismounted, and inquired of his squaw if he was at home. She sent her little girl out into the field to call him. There, indeed, in his cornfield, was he at work. He met me very cordially; and invited me into a room, where he had an interpretor. We held a protracted and agreeable conversation on Indian matters. He invited me to dine with him, and nothing but want of time prevented my accepting his polite invitation. He was very neatly dressed, and is quite prepossessing in his appearance. He is younger than I supposed before seeing him. I judge him to be about thirty-four. He is a man of strong sense, of great sagacity, and considerable ambition.

There is no reason why the Indians should not speedily become civilized. Those who have longest lived amongst them, and who best understand their character, tell me so. I fully believe it. The Indian follows his wild habits because he has been educated to do so. The education of habit, familiar from infancy, and the influence of tradition, lead him to the hunt, and as much to despise manual labor. He does what he has been taught to consider as noble and honorable, and that is what the most enlightened do. Certainly his course of life is the most severe and exposed; it is not for comfort that he adheres to his wild habits. He regards it as noble to slay his hereditary foe. Hence the troubles which occasionally break out between the Chippewas and the Sioux. To gain the applause of their tribe they will incur almost any danger, and undergo almost any privation. Thus, we see that for those objects which their education has taught them to regard as first and best, they will sacrifice all their comforts. They have sense enough, and ambition enough, and fortitude enough. To those they love they are affectionate almost to excess. Only direct their ambition in the proper way, and they will at once rise. Teach them that it is noble to produce something useful by their labor, and to unite with the great family of man to expand arts and to improve the immortal mind — teach them that it is noble, that there is more applause to be gained by it, as well as comfort, and they will change in a generation. They will then apply themselves to civilization with Spartan zeal and with Spartan virtues.

In a communication to the secretary of war by Gen. Cass in 1821, relative to his expedition to the sources of the Mississippi, he makes the following interesting extract from the journal of Mr. Doty, a gentleman who accompanied the expedition:— "The Indians of the upper country consider those of the Fond-du-Lac as very stupid and dull, being but little given to war. They count the Sioux their enemies, but have heretofore made few war excursions.

"Having been frequently reprimanded by some of the more vigilant Indians of the north, and charged with cowardice, and an utter disregard for the event of the war, thirteen men of this tribe, last season, determined to retrieve the character of their nation, by making an excursion against the Sioux. Accordingly, without consulting the other Indians, they secretly departed and penetrated far into the Sioux country. Unexpectedly, at night, they came upon a party of the Sioux, amounting to near one hundred men, and immediately began to prepare for battle. They encamped a short distance from the Sioux, and during the night dug holes in the ground into which they might retreat and fight to the last extremity. They appointed one of their number (the youngest) to take a station at a distance and witness the struggle, and instructed him, when they were all slain, to make his escape to their own land, and relate the circumstances under which they had fallen.

"Early in the morning they attacked the Sioux in their camp, who, immediately sallying out upon them, forced them back to the last place of retreat they had resolved upon. They fought desperately. More than twice their own number were killed before they had lost their lives. Eight of them were tomahawked in the holes to which they had retreated; the other four fell on the field. The thirteenth returned home, according to the directions he had received, and related the foregoing circumstances to his tribe. They mourned their death; but delighted with the bravery of their friends, unexampled in modern times, they were happy in their grief.

"This account I received of the very Indian who was of the party and had escaped." — [See Schoolcraft, p. 481.][1]

[1 Pride is a characteristic trait in Indian character. On a recent occasion when several bands of the Chippewas were at Washington to negotiate a treaty with the United States, they had an interview with their Great Father the President. He received them in the spacious East Room of the executive mansion, in the presence of a large collection of gentlemen who had gathered to witness the occasion. Each chief made a speech to the President, which was interpreted as they spoke. When it came to the turn of *Eshkibogikoj* (Flat Mouth) that venerable chief began with great dignity, saying: "Father! *Two great men have met!*" Here he paused to let the sentence be interpreted. His exordium amused not only the whites but the Indians.]

In the contest between the Athenians and the Dorians, an oracle had declared that the side would triumph whose king should fall. Codrus the Athenian king, to be more sure of sacrificing himself, assumed the dress of a peasant, and was soon killed; and the event soon spread dismay among the enemies of Athens. His patriotism was accounted so great, that the Athenians declared that there was no man worthy to be his successor, and so abolished the monarchy. I think the history of the Indians would show instances of heroism as praiseworthy as can be found in the annals of the ancients. Let it be remembered, too, that the Spartans knew that an imperishable literature would hand down their valor to the praise of the world through all the future. But the Indian looked for the preservation of his exploits only in the songs and the traditional stories of his tribe.

I allude to these traits because I think it will be agreed, that whatever race possesses those elements of character which lead them to pursue with zeal and courage things they have been taught to regard most creditable, is capable of being civilized. We now pay the Indian for his lands in agricultural tools, in muskets and powder, in blankets and cheap calico — and in education; but the smallest item is education. If half the money which the government is liable to pay for Indian troubles during the last year, could be appropriated to a proper system of education, we should hear of no more serious Indian wars. But I have not time to pursue the subject. I will say, however, that the present commissioner of Indian affairs, Mr. Manypenny, is doing a very good work in advancing their condition. The press ought to bestow some attention on the subject. There are nearly 400,000 Indians within the United States and territories. If the philanthropy of the age could spare the blacks for a little while, and help civilize the Indians, it would be better for all parties. Here is an enterprise for genuine humanity.

LETTER VIII.

LUMBERING INTERESTS.

Lumber as an element of wealth — Quality of Minnesota lumber — Locality of its growth — The great pineries — Trespasses on government land — How the lumbermen elude the government — Value of lumber — Character of the practical Lumberman — Transportation of lumber on rafts.

CROW WING, October 1856.

IT seems to have been more difficult for countries which abound in precious metals to attain to great prosperity than for a rich man to secure eternal felicity. Witness, for instance, the sluggish growth and degenerate civilization of the South American states. But timber is a fundamental element of colonial growth. The mines of Potosi cannot compare with it in value. An abundance of timber and a superabundance of it are two very different things. Some of the Middle, and what were once Western States, were originally covered with forests. So of the greater part of New England. In Ohio and in Michigan timber has been an encumbrance; for there was great labor to be performed by the settler in clearing the land and preparing it for the plough; and at this day we see in travelling through each of those states, as well as in Kentucky, Tennessee, and Missouri, fields planted amidst heavy timber trees which have been belted that they may wither and die. By an abundance of timber I mean an ample supply not only for domestic but foreign market; and with this understanding of the word I will repeat what has often been said, and what I suppose is well known, that Minnesota has an abundance of excellent timber. Unlike the gorgeous forests in New Hampshire, which behind high cliffs and mountain fastnesses defy the woodman, the timber of Minnesota grows in the valleys of her great rivers and upon the banks of their numerous tributaries. It is thus easily shipped to a distant market; while the great body of the land, not encumbered with it, but naked, is ready for the plough and for the seed. Most of the timber which grows in the region below this point is hard wood, such as elm, maple, oak, and ash.

There is considerable scrub oak also thinly scattered over large portions of fertile prairie. To a casual observer these oaks, from their stunted appearance, would be taken as evidence of poor soil. But the soil is not the cause of their scrubby looks. It is the devouring fires which annually sweep over the plains with brilliant though terrific aspect, and which are fed by the luxuriant grass grown on that same soil. If the oaks did not draw uncommon nourishment from the soil, it must be difficult for them to survive such scorchings. It is a consoling thought that these fires cease in proportion as the country is settled up. The rock maple is indigenous to the soil; and the Indians have long been in the habit of making sugar from its sap. The timber most used for fences is tamarack. The pineries may be said to begin at the mouth of the Crow Wing River; though there is a great supply on the Rum River. For upwards of a hundred miles above here on the Mississippi— more or less dense, the pine forests extend. Captain John Pope, in the interesting report of his expedition to the Red River of the North, in 1849, says— " The pineries of the upper Mississippi are mostly upon its tributaries, and I think are not found on the west side further south than the parallel of 46 degrees N. latitude." (The latitude of this place is 46 degrees 16' 50".) "They alternate, even where most abundant, with much larger tracts of fertile country." Again he says— "As might be expected from its alluvial character, there is no pine timber in the valley of the Red River, but the oak and elm there attain to a size which I do not think I have ever seen elsewhere." In another place he remarks that "the pineries along the Crow Wing River are among the most extensive and valuable found on the tributaries of the Mississippi." Mr. Schoolcraft says of this river, "the whole region is noted for its pine timber." In speaking of the country on the St. Louis River, a few miles from where it empties into Lake Superior, the same gentleman remarks: "The growth of the forest is pines, hemlock, spruce, birch, oak, and maple." I had heard considerable about Minnesota lumber, it is true, but I was not prepared to see the pine timber so valuable and heavy as it is above and about here. The trees are of large growth, straight and smooth. They are not surpassed by

> "The tallest pine, Hewn on Norwegian hills to be the mast Of some great admiral."

Cujus est solum ejus est usque ad caelum— whose the soil, his to the sky— is a maxim in these pine regions of literal importance. There is something besides utility also to be mentioned in this connection. With the exception of swamps, which are few and far between, the timber land has all the beauty of a sylvan grove. The entire absence of underbrush and decayed logs lends ornament and attraction to the woods. They are more like the groves around a mansion in their neat and cheerful appearance; and awaken reflection on the Muses and the dialogues of philosophers rather than apprehension of wild beasts and serpents.

The relative importance of the lumber business would hardly be estimated by a stranger. It has been carried on for at least six years; and considerable has found its way as far down as St. Louis. It will be asked, I imagine, if all this timber land, especially the pine, has been sold by the government; and if not, how it happens that men cut it down and sell it? I will answer this. The great region of pineries has not yet been surveyed, much less sold by the government. But notwithstanding this, men have cut it in large quantities, sold it into a greedy market, and made money, if not fortunes in the business. As a sort of colorable excuse for cutting timber, those employed in the business often make a preemption claim on land covered with it, and many people suppose they have the right to cut as much as they please after the incipient steps towards preemption. But this is not so. All that a claimant can do in this respect is to cut wood enough for his fuel, and timber enough for his own building purposes, until he receives a patent from the government. Of course it is altogether reasonable and proper that men should be precluded from doing so until their title in the soil is complete. Because, until a preemption claim is perfect, or, until the land has been acquired by some legal title, it is not certain that the claimant will ultimately secure it or pay any money to the government. But does not the government do anything to prevent these trespasses? Yes, but all its attempts are baffled.

For example, last spring a large quantity of splendid lumber was seized by the United States marshal and sold at public auction. It was bid off by the lumbermen themselves, who had formed a combination to prevent its falling into the hands of other purchasers. This combination had no resistance as I am aware of in the public opinion of the territory, and the timber was sold to those who had it cut at a price so far below its value that it didn't pay the expense of the legal proceedings on the part of the government. This is accounted for in the fact of the exhaustless quantity of pine timber towards the north; in the demand for it when sawed; and in the disposition to protect enterprising men, though technically trespassers, who penetrate into the forest in the winter at great expense, and whose standing and credit are some guaranty of their ultimate responsibility to the government, should they not perfect their titles. The business of getting out the timber is carried on in the winter, and affords employment for a large number of athletic young men. The price of timber, I ascertained of Mr. P. D. Pratt, a dealer at St. Paul, is, for the best, $30 per M.; for common, $20.

Most people have seen or been told something of the lumbermen of Maine. Allowing this to be so, it will not be difficult to comprehend the condition and character of the lumbermen of Minnesota and the northwest. But if there is anybody who fancies them to be a set of laborers, such as build our railroads and dig coal and minerals, he is greatly mistaken. The difference is in birth and education; between foreigners and native-born citizens. A difference not in rights and merits, so much as in habits and character. Born on American soil, they have attended our common schools, and have the bearing and independence of sovereigns. None but very vigorous men can endure, or at least attempt to endure, the exposure of living in the woods all winter and swinging the axe; though by proper care of themselves, such exercise is conducive to health and strength. Accordingly we find the lumberman— I mean of course the practical lumberman— to be a thick-set, muscular young man, with a bright eye and florid cheek; in short, one whom we would call a double-fisted fellow. He is not one of your California boys, but more affable and domestic, with a shorter beard, and not so great a profusion of weapons. His dress is snug and plain— the regular pioneer costume of boots over the pants, and a thick red shirt in lieu of a coat. His capital stock is his health and his hands. When in employment he is economical and lays up his wages. When out of employment and in town, his money generally goes freely. As a class, the lumbermen are intelligent. They are strong talkers, for they put in a good many of the larger sort of words; and from their pungent satire and sledge-hammer style of reasoning, are by no means very facile disputants. They are preeminently jokers. This is as they appear on their way to the woods. During the season of their active labor they usually spend the evening, after a day of hard work, in storytelling or in a game of euchre. Their wages amount to about two dollars a day, exclusive of board. They have good living in the woods, the provisions, which are furnished on an ample scale, being served by male cooks.

While on the subject of lumber, which may possibly interest some people who wish to redeem the fortunes they have lately lost in Maine lumber, I ought not to leave unmentioned the valuable cargoes of it which are floated down the Mississippi. When coming up in the boat I was astonished to see such stupendous rafts. Large logs are transported by being made into rafts. At a landing where the boat stopped, I on one occasion attempted to estimate the number of logs comprised in one of these marine novelties, and found it to be about eight hundred; the logs were large, and were worth from five to six dollars each. Here then was a raft of timber worth at least $4000. They are navigated by about a dozen men, with large paddles attached at either end of the raft, which serve to propel and steer. Often, in addition to the logs, the rafts are laden with valuable freights of sawed lumber. Screens are built as a protection against wind, and a caboose stands somewhere in the centre, or according to western parlance it might be called a cabin. Sometimes the raft will be running in a fine current; then only a couple of hands are on the watch and at the helm. The rest are seen either loitering about observing the country, or reclining, snugly wrapped up in their blankets. Some of these rafts must cover as much as two acres. Birnam Wood coming to Dunsinane was not a much greater phenomenon.

LETTER IX.

SHORES OF LAKE SUPERIOR.

Description of the country around Lake Superior— Minerals— Locality of a commercial city— New land districts— Buchanan— Ojibeway— Explorations to the sources of the Mississippi— Henry R. Schoolcraft— M. Nicollet's report— Resources of the country above Crow Wing.

CROW WING, October 7, 1856.

THERE is one very important section of this territory that I have not yet alluded to. I mean that part which borders on Lake Superior. This calls to mind that there is such a place as Superior City. But that is in Wisconsin, not in Minnesota. From that city (so called, yet city in earnest it is like to be) to the nearest point in this territory the distance by water is twelve miles. The St. Louis River is the dividing line for many miles between Minnesota and Wisconsin. The country round about this greatest of inland seas is not the most fertile. It is somewhat bleak, on the northern shore especially, but is nevertheless fat in minerals. On the banks of the St. Louis River the soil is described, by the earliest explorers as well as latest visiters, to be good. The river itself, though it contains a large volume of water, is not adapted to navigation, on account of its rapids.

Those who have sailed across Lake Superior to the neighborhood of Fond-du-Lac appear to have been charmed by the scenery of its magnificent islands and its rock-bound shores. Most people, I suppose, have heard of its beautiful cluster of islands called the Twelve Apostles. One peculiar phenomenon often mentioned is the boisterous condition of its waters at the shore, which occurs when the lake itself is perfectly calm. The water is said to foam and dash so furiously as to make it almost perilous to land in a small boat. This would seem to be produced by some movement of the waters similar to the flow of the tide; and perhaps the dashing after all is not much more tumultuous than is seen on a summer afternoon under the rocks of Nahant, or along the serene coast at Phillips Beach.

The resources of that part of the territory bordering on the lake, however, are sufficient to induce an extensive, if not a rapid, settlement of the country. The copper mines afford occupation for thousands of people now. I have known a young man to clear $40 a month in getting out the ore. But the labor is hard. Somewhere near Fond-du-Lac is destined to be a great commercial city. Whether it will be at Superior, which has now got the start of all other places, or whether it will be at some point within this territory, is more than can be known at present. But a great town there is to be, sooner or later; and for this reason, that the distance from Buffalo to Fond-du-Lac by navigation is about the same as from Buffalo to Chicago, affording, therefore, as good facilities for water transportation of merchandise between Fond-du-Lac and the East, as between Chicago and the East. Moreover, the development of this new agricultural world will tend to that result. A railroad will then run from that point directly west, crossing the upper Mississippi as also the Red River of the North at the head of its navigation, which is at the mouth of the Sioux Wood River.

During the last summer, congress established two new land districts in the upper part of the territory, called the north-eastern and the north-western. The former includes the country lying on Lake Superior, and its land office has been located at Buchanan, a new place just started on the shore of the lake. The land office for the north-western district has been located at Ojibeway, a town site situated sixty miles above here, on the Mississippi, near the mouth of Muddy River. This district includes the head waters of the Mississippi, and extends west as far as the Red River of the North. The surveyors have been engaged in either district only a few weeks. I don't expect there will be any land offered for sale in either district till spring. While on the subject of land offices, let me observe that the appointments in them are among the most lucrative under the patronage of the general government. There is a register and receiver for each office. They have, each, $500 per annum and fees; the whole not to exceed $3000. Aside from the official fees, they get much more for private services. They have more or less evidence to reduce to writing in nearly every preemption case, for which the general land office permits them to receive private compensation. It is rather necessary that the local land officers should be lawyers, as they have frequent occasion to decide on litigated land claims.

Many explorations have been made of the region around the head waters of the Mississippi, the reports of which have conveyed to the world attractive information of the country, but information which only approximated to accuracy. In 1806, Lieut. Pike explored the river as far as Turtle Lake, and returned, thinking, good easy man, full surely he had discovered the real source of the river, and yet the source of the river was more than a hundred miles off in another direction. Lewis and Clarke had ascended the river previously. In 1820, General Cass, accompanied by Mr. Schoolcraft, explored the river to Cass Lake; being obliged to stop there on account of the low stage of water which they heard existed a few days' journey beyond. Again, in 1832, Mr. Schoolcraft, then superintendent of Indian affairs, made another expedition, which resulted in his discovery of the true sources of the river; it being a lake which he named *Itasca*. It has been said that he manufactured this beautiful word out of the last syllables of *veritas* and the first syllable of *caput* (the true head). But I have been told that the word was suggested to his mind by an Indian word signifying breast. Dr. Johnson says, that a traveller in order to bring back knowledge should take knowledge with him. That is, that he should have posted himself up to some extent on the country he visits. I hope it will not require an affidavit for me to prove that I availed myself of the suggestion. But I must say I have found great pleasure and profit in perusing Mr. Schoolcraft's narratives of both his expeditions. Though he had the encouragement of the government, his undertaking was surrounded by many obstacles and some dangers. His account of the whole country is pleasant and instructive to the reader, and shows that all he saw produced on his mind a favorable impression. The arduous services of this gentleman as an explorer have been of great advantage to the country, and his fine literary talents have given his adventures an historic fame. Not less deserving of applause either have been his efforts to promote the welfare of the Indians. He now lives in affluent circumstances at Washington, and, though suffering under some bodily infirmities, appears (or did when I saw him) to enjoy life with that serene and rational happiness which springs from useful employment, and a consciousness that past opportunities have been improved.

> "For he lives twice who can at once employ
> The present well and e'en the past enjoy."

There have been other explorations of this part of the country at different times by Messrs. Long, Nicollet, and Pope. M. Nicollet was accompanied and assisted by Mr. (then Lieutenant) Fremont. The reports made of these explorations afford information which, if extensively known among the people, would tend to direct a larger emigration into the upper part of the territory. They often launch off into exclamations as to the beautiful surface of the country; while their account of native fruits and the bracing climate and fertile soil picture to the imagination all the elements of a home.

M. Nicollet was a foreign gentleman who possessed superior scientific knowledge and a rare zeal to prosecute researches. He made an exploration through the valley of the St. Peter's and the Missouri; and from thence to the sources of the Mississippi, in the year 1839. The official report which he made is a valuable document, but difficult to be obtained. I shall therefore make a few extracts from it. I should here remark that M. Nicollet died before he had completed the introduction to his report. "The Mississippi," he says, "holds its own from its very origin; for it is not necessary to suppose, as has been done, that Lake Itasca may be supplied with invisible sources, to justify the character of a remarkable stream, which it assumes at its issue from this lake. There are five creeks that fall into it, formed by innumerable streamlets oozing from the clay-beds at the bases of the hills, that consist of an accumulation of sand, gravel, and clay, intermixed with erratic fragments; being a more prominent portion of the great erratic deposit previously described, and which here is known by the name of '*Hauteurs des Terres*' — heights of land.

"These elevations are commonly flat at top, varying in height from 85 to 100 feet above the level of the surrounding waters. They are covered with thick forests, in which coniferous plants predominate. South of Itasca Lake, they form a semicircular region with a boggy bottom, extending to the south-west a distance of several miles; thence these *Hauteurs des Terres* ascend to the north-west and north; and then, stretching to the north-east and east, through the zone between 47 degrees and 48 degrees of latitude, make the dividing ridge between the waters that empty into Hudson's Bay and those which discharge themselves into the Gulf of Mexico. The principal group of these *Hauteurs des Terres* is subdivided into several ramifications, varying in extent, elevation, and course, so as to determine the hydrographical basins of all the innumerable lakes and rivers that so peculiarly characterize this region of country.

"One of these ramifications extends in a southerly direction under the name of *Coteau du Grand Bois;* and it is this which separates the Mississippi streams from those of the Red River of the North.

"The waters supplied by the north flank of these heights of land — still on the south side of Lake Itasca — give origin to the five creeks of which I have spoken above. These are the waters which I consider to be the utmost sources of the Mississippi. Those that flow from the southern side of the same heights, and empty themselves into Elbow Lake, are the utmost sources of the Red River of the North; so that the most remote feeders of Hudson's Bay and the Gulf of Mexico are closely approximated to each other."

Of the country above Crow Wing, he makes the following observations, which are not less interesting than instructive: "Over the whole route which I traversed after leaving Crow Wing River, the country has a different aspect from that which the banks of the Mississippi above the falls present. The forests are denser and more varied; the soil, which is alternately sandy, gravelly, clayey, and loamy, is, generally speaking, lighter excepting on the shores of some of the larger lakes. The uplands are covered with white and yellow pines, spruce and birch; and the wet lowlands by the American larch and the willow. On the slopes of sandy hills, the American aspen, the canoe birch (white birch), with a species of birch of dwarfish growth, the alder, and wild rose, extend to the very margin of the river. On the borders of the larger lakes, where the soil is generally better, we find the sugar maple, the black and bar oaks (also named overcup white oak, but differing from the white oak), the elm, ash, lime tree, &c. Generally speaking, however, this woodland does not extend back farther than a mile from the lakes. The white cedar, the hemlock, spruce, pine, and fir, are occasionally found; but the red cedar is scarce throughout this region, and none, perhaps, are to be seen but on islands of those lakes called by the Indians Red Cedar Lakes. The shrubbery consists principally of the wild rose, hawthorn, and wild plum; and raspberries, blackberries, strawberries, and cranberries are abundant.

"The aspect of the country is greatly varied by hills, dales, copses, small prairies, and a great number of lakes; the whole of which I do not pretend to have laid down on my map. * * * * The lakes to which I have just alluded are distributed in separate groups, or are arranged in prolonged chains along the rivers, and not unfrequently attached to each other by gentle rapids. It has seemed to me that they diminish in extent on both sides of the Mississippi, as we proceed southwardly, as far as 43 degrees of north latitude; and this observation extends to the Arctic region, commencing at Bear's Lake; or Slave Lake, Winnipeg Lake, &c. It may be further remarked that the basins of these lakes have a sufficient depth to leave no doubt that they will remain characteristic features of the country for a long time to come. Several species of fish abound in them. The white fish *(Corregonus albus)* is found in all the deep lakes west of the Mississippi— and, indeed, from Lake Erie to the Polar Sea. That which is taken in Leech Lake is said by amateurs to be more highly flavored than even that of Lake Superior, and weighs from three to ten pounds.* * * Of all the Indian nations that I have visited, the Chippewas, inhabiting the country about the sources of the Mississippi, are decidedly the most favored. Besides their natural resources (to which I have already referred) of fish, wild rice, and maple sugar, with the addition of an abundance of game, the climate is found to be well adapted to the culture of corn, wheat, barley, oats, and pulse. The potato is of superior quality to that of the Middle States of the Union. In a trading point of view, the hunt is very profitable. The bear, the deer and elk, the wolf, the fox, the wolverine, the fisher raccoon, muskrat, mink, otter, marten, weasel, and a few remaining beavers, are the principal articles of this traffic." (pp. 58, 64.) To those who are desirous of perusing this valuable report, and who have access to the congressional documents, I would say that it may be found in Senate Document 237, 2d Session of 26th Congress.

LETTER X.

VALLEY OF THE RED RIVER OF THE NORTH.

Climate of Minnesota — The settlement at Pembina — St. Joseph — Col. Smith's expedition — Red River of the North — Fur trade — Red River Settlement — The Hudson's Bay Company — Ex-Gov. Ramsey's observations — Dacotah.

CROW WING, October, 1856.

A CELEBRATED geographer of the first century wrote, "Germany is indeed habitable, but is uninhabited on account of the cold." I am not so certain, but some people have a similar idea of the upper portion of Minnesota. If there are any, however, thus distrustful of its climate, they probably live out of the territory. I have no means of knowing what the climate is here in winter, except from hearsay and general principles. It seems to be an approved theory, that the farther we approach the west in a northern latitude the milder becomes the winter. The stage-drivers tell me that the snow does not fall to such a depth as in the northern part of New England; that the weather is tolerably uniform; and that the roads are at all times kept open and much travelled. After all, it is a great way before we come to the home of the Esquimaux, and the desert of ice where Sir John Franklin perished.

I will here subjoin the following extract from a letter addressed to Gov. Stephens by the Hon. Henry M. Rice, the able delegate from Minnesota. It is dated 3d June, 1854:

"Navigation of the Mississippi River closes from the 10th to the 25th of November, and opens from the 1st to the 10th of April. That of the Red River of the North closes from the 1st to 16th November, and opens from 10th to 25th April. I have often travelled in the winter from St. Paul to Crow Wing, a distance of one hundred and fifty miles, with a single horse and sled, without a track, and have never found the snow deep enough to impede my progress. I have also gone from Crow Wing, beyond the head waters of the Mississippi, to the waters of the Hudson's Bay, on foot and without snow-shoes. I spent one entire winter travelling through that region, and never found the snow over eighteen inches deep, and seldom over nine inches.

"For several years I had trading-posts extending from Lake Superior to the Red River of the North, from 46 degrees to 49 degrees north latitude, and never found the snow so deep as to prevent supplies being transported from one post to another with horses. One winter, north of Crow Wing, say 47 degrees north latitude, I wintered about sixty head of horses and cattle without giving them food of any kind except such as they could procure themselves under the snow. Between the 45th and 49th degrees north latitude, the snow does not fall so deep as it does between the 40th and 45th degrees; this is easily accounted for upon the same principle that in the fall they have frosts much earlier near the 40th than they do near the 45th degree. I say this in reference to the country watered by the Mississippi River. Owing to its altitude the atmosphere is dry beyond belief, which accounts for the absence of frosts in the fall, and for the small quantity of snow that falls in a country so far north. Voyageurs traverse the territory from Lake Superior to the Missouri the entire winter with horses and sleds, having to make their own roads, and yet with heavy loads are not detained by snow. Lumbermen in great numbers winter in the pine regions of Minnesota with their teams, and I have never heard of their finding the snow too deep to prosecute their labors. I have known several winters when the snow at no time was over six inches deep."

The Hon. H. H. Sibley, ex-delegate from Minnesota, in a letter dated at Mendota says: "As our country is for the most part composed of prairie, it is of course much exposed to the action of the winds. It is, however, a peculiarity of our climate, that calms prevail during the cold weather of the winter months; consequently, the snow does not drift to anything like the extent experienced in New England or northern New York. I have never believed that railroad communication in this territory would be seriously impeded by the depth or drift of snow, unless, perhaps, in the extreme northern portion of it." (See Explorations and Surveys for the Pacific Railroad, I., 400.)

A few facts in regard to the people who live four or five hundred miles to the north, will best illustrate the nature of the climate and its adaptedness to agriculture.

It is common to say that settlements have not extended beyond Crow Wing. This is only technically true. There is a settlement at Pembina, where the dividing line between British America and the United States crosses the Red River of the North. It didn't *extend* there from our frontier, sure enough. If it extended from anywhere it must have been from the north, or along the confines of that mystic region called Rainy Lake. Pembina is said to have about 600 inhabitants. It is situated on the Pembina River. It is an Indian-French word meaning cranberry. Men live there who were born there, and it is in fact an old settlement. It was founded by British subjects, who thought they had located on British soil. The greater part of its inhabitants are half-breeds, who earn a comfortable livelihood in fur hunting and in farming. It sends two representatives and a councillor to the territorial legislature. It is 460 miles north-west of St. Paul, and 330 miles distant from this town. Notwithstanding the distance, there is considerable communication between the places. West of Pembina, about thirty miles, is a settlement called St. Joseph, situated N. of a large mythological body of water called Miniwakan, or Devil's Lake; and is one of the points where Col. Smith's expedition was intending to stop. This expedition to which I refer, started out from Fort Snelling in the summer, to explore the country on both sides of the Red River of the North as far as Pembina, and to report to the war department the best points for the establishment of a new military post. It is expected that Col. Smith will return by the first of next month; and it is probable he will advise the erection of a post at Pembina. When that is done, if it is done, its effect will be to draw emigrants from the Red River settlement into Minnesota.

Now let me say a word about this Red River of the North, for it is beginning to be a great feature in this upper country. It runs north, and empties into Lake Winnipeg, which connects with Hudson's Bay by Nelson River. It is a muddy and sluggish stream, navigable to the mouth of Sioux Wood River for vessels of three feet draught for four months in the year. So that the extent of its navigation within the territory alone (between Pembina and the mouth of Sioux Wood River) is 417 miles. Buffaloes still feed on its western banks. Its tributaries are numerous and copious, abounding with the choicest kinds of game, and skirted with a various and beautiful foliage. It cannot be many years before this magnificent valley shall pour its products into our markets, and be the theatre of a busy and genial life.

One of the first things which drew my attention to this river was a sight of several teams travelling towards this vicinity from a north-westerly direction. I observed that the complexion of those in the caravan was a little darker than that of pure white Minnesotians, and that the carts were a novelty. "Who are those people? and where are they from?" I inquired of a friend. "They are Red River people, just arrived — they have come down to trade." Their carts are made to be drawn by one animal, either an ox or a horse, and are put together without the use of a particle of iron. They are excellently adapted to prairie travelling. How strange it seems! Here are people who have been from twenty to thirty days on their journey to the nearest civilized community. This is their nearest market. Their average rate of travelling is about fifteen miles a day, and they generally secure game enough on the way for their living. I have had highly interesting accounts of the Red River settlement since I have been here, both from Mr. Ross and Mr. Marion, gentlemen recently from there. The settlement is seventy miles north of Pembina, and lies on both sides of the river. Its population is estimated at 10,000. It owes its origin and growth to the enterprise and success of the Hudson's Bay Company. Many of the settlers came from Scotland, but the most were from Canada. They speak English and Canadian French. The English style of society is well kept up, whether we regard the church with its bishop, the trader with his wine cellar, the scholar with his library, the officer with his sinecure, or their paper currency. I find they have everything but a hotel, for I was particular on that point, though not intending just yet to go there. Probably the arrivals do not justify such an institution, but their cordial hospitality will make up for any such lack, from all I hear. They have a judge who gets a good house to live in, and L1000 sterling a year; but he has nothing of consequence to do. He was formerly a leading lawyer in Canada.

The great business of the settlement, of course, is the fur traffic. An immense amount of buffalo skins is taken in the summer and autumn, while in the winter smaller but more valuable furs are procured. The Indians also enlist in the hunts; and it is estimated that upwards of $200,000 worth of furs are annually taken from our territory and sold to the Hudson's Bay Company. It is high time indeed that a military post should be established somewhere on the Red River by our government. The Hudson's Bay Company is now a powerful monopoly. Not so magnificent and potent as the East India Company, it is still a powerful combination, showering opulence on its members, and reflecting a peculiar feature in the strength and grandeur of the British empire— a power, which, to use the eloquent language of Daniel Webster, "has dotted over the whole surface of the globe with her possessions and military posts— whose morning drum-beat, following the sun, and keeping company with the hours, circles the earth daily with one continuous and unbroken strain of martial music." The company is growing richer every year, and its jurisdiction and its lands will soon find an availability never dreamed of by its founders, unless, as may possibly happen, popular sovereignty steps in to grasp the fruits of its long apprenticeship. Some time ago I believe the Canadas sought to annex this broad expanse to their own jurisdiction. There are about two hundred members in the Hudson's Bay Company. The charter gives them the power to legislate for the settlement. They have many persons in their employ in England as well as in British America. A clerk, after serving the company ten years, with a salary of about $500 per annum, is considered qualified for membership, with the right to vote in the deliberations of the company, and one share in the profits. The profits of a share last year amounted to

$10,000! A factor of the company, after serving ten years, is entitled to membership with the profits of two shares. The aristocracy of the settlement consists principally of retired factors and other members of the company, who possess large fortunes, dine on juicy roast beef, with old port, ride in their carriages, and enjoy life in a very comfortable manner. Two of the company's ships sail up into Hudson's Bay every year to bring merchandise to the settlement and take away furs. [1] But the greatest portion of the trade is done with Minnesota. Farming is carried on in the neighborhood of the settlement with cheerful ease and grand success. I was as much surprised to hear of the nature of their agriculture as of anything else concerning the settlement. The same kind of crops are raised as in Pennsylvania or Maine; and this in a country, be it remembered, five hundred miles and upwards north of St. Paul. Stock must be easily raised, as it would appear from the fact that it is driven down here into the territory and sold at a great profit. Since I have been here, a drove of fine-looking cattle from that settlement passed to be sold in the towns below, and a drove of horses is expected this fall. The stock which comes from there is more hardy than can be got anywhere else, and therefore is preferred by the Minnesotians.

[1 "The Hudson's Bay Company allows its servants, while making a voyage, eight pounds of meat a day, and I am told the allowance is none too much." (Lieutenant Howison's Report on Oregon, p. 7.)]

The following extract from Ex-Governor Ramsey's address, recently delivered before the annual fair at Minneapolis, wherein he gives some results of his observations of the Red River settlement during his trip there in 1851, will be read with much interest: —

"Re-embarking in our canoes, we continued descending the river for some fifteen miles further, through the French portion of the settlement, lining mainly the west or left bank of the river, until we arrived about the centre of the colony, at the mouth of the Assinniboin tributary of Red River, where we landed and remained a few days, viewing the colony and its improvements. I was at that time, and am even now, when I look back upon it, lost in wonder at the phenomena which that settlement exhibits to the world, considering its location in an almost polar region of the North. Imagine a river flowing sluggishly northward through a flat alluvial plain, and the west side of it lined continuously for over thirty miles with cultivated farms, each presenting those appearances of thrift around them which I mentioned as surrounding the first farms seen by us; but each farm with a narrow frontage on the river of only twenty-four rods in width, but extending back for one or two miles, and each of these narrow farms having their dwellings and the farm out-buildings spread only along the river front, with lawns sloping to the water's edge, and shrubbery and vines liberally trained around them, and trees intermingled— the whole presenting the appearance of a long suburban village— such as you might see near our eastern sea-board, or such as you find exhibited in pictures of English country villages, with the resemblance rendered more striking by the spires of several large churches peeping above the foliage of the trees in the distance, whitewashed school-houses glistening here and there amidst sunlight and green; gentlemen's houses of pretentious dimensions and grassy lawns and elaborate fencing, the seats of retired officers of the Hudson's Bay Company occasionally interspersed; here an English bishop's parsonage, with a boarding or high school near by; and over there a Catholic bishop's massive cathedral, with a convent of Sisters of Charity attached; whilst the two large stone forts, at which reside the officers of the Hudson's Bay Company, or of the colony once called Upper Fort Garry, and situated at the mouth of the Assinniboin, and the other termini the Lower Fort Garry, which is twenty miles farther down the river, helped to give additional picturesqueness to the scene. I had almost forgotten to mention what is, after all, the most prominent and peculiar feature of that singular landscape, singular from its location— and that is the numerous wind-mills, nearly twenty in all, which on every point of land made by the turns and bends in the river, stretched out their huge sails athwart the horizon, and seemingly looked defiance at us as invading strangers, that were from a land where steam or water mills monopolize their avocation of flour making. One morning as we passed down the principal high road, on our way to Lower Fort Garry, the wind, after a protracted calm, began to blow a little; when presto! each mill veered around its sails to catch the propitious breeze, and as the sails began to revolve, it was curious to observe the numerous carts that shot out from nearly every farm-house, and hurried along the road to these mills, to get ground their grists of spring wheat, with which they were respectively loaded.

"Another incident during the same trip that struck us oddly, was seeing two ladies driving by themselves a fine horse hitched to a buggy of modern fashion, just as much at home apparently as if they were driving through the streets of St. Paul, or St. Anthony, or Minneapolis, instead of upon that remote highway towards the North Pole; but this was not a whit more novel than to hear the pianoforte, and played, too, with both taste and skill. While another 'lion' of those parts that met our view was a topsail schooner lying in the river at the lower fort, which made occasional trips into Great Lake Winnepeg of the North, a hundred miles below.

"I took occasion during my visit to inquire what success the farmers met with in securing good crops, and the profits of farmers generally. As to wheat, I learned that the yield of the spring variety was quite equal in quantity and quality to the crop of that grain on any more southern farms; that in raising barley they could almost surpass the world; and the cereals generally, and all the esculent roots, were easily raised. Indian corn was not planted as a field crop, though it was grown in their gardens. In a word, the capacity of their land to produce almost everything plentifully and well, was established; but for all this, farming did not afford much profit. for want of a sufficient market; beyond a small demand by the Hudson's Bay Company, there was no outlet for their superabundance; and to use an Austrian phase in regard to Hungarians, the Selkirkers are metaphysically 'smothering in their own fat.' To remedy this state of things they were beginning, when I was there, to turn their attention towards raising cattle and horses, for which their country is well calculated; and the first fruits of this new decision given to their farming energies, we have already experienced in the droves of both which have recently been driven from thence and sold in this vicinity."

I think the facts which I have herein hastily set downhill dispel any apprehension as to the successful cultivation of the soil in the northern part of the territory. It has a health-giving climate which before long, I predict, will nourish as patriotic a race of men as gave immortality to the noble plains of Helvetia. There is one thing I would mention which seems to auspicate the speedy development of the valley of the North Red River. Next year Minnesota will probably be admitted as a state; and a new territory organized out of the broad region embracing the valley aforesaid and the head waters of the Mississippi. Or else it will be divided by a line north and south, including the western valley of that river, and extending as far to the west as the Missouri River. I understand it will be called Dacotah, though I at first thought it would be called Pembina. There is always a rush into new territories, and the proposed new territory of Dacotah will present sufficient inducements for a large immigration. When the valley of the North Red River shall be settled, and splendid harvest fields adorn its banks; when great factories take the place of wind-mills, and when railroads shall take the place of Red River carts, then we will have new cause to exclaim,

"Westward the course of empire takes its way!"

LETTER XI.

THE TRUE PIONEER.

Energy of the pioneer— Frontier life— Spirit of emigration— Advantages to the farmer in moving West— Advice in regard to making preemption claims— Abstract of the preemption law— Hints to the settler— Character and services of the pioneer.

CROW WING, October, 1856.

I DESIRE in this letter to say something about the pioneer, and life on the frontier. And by pioneer I mean the true pioneer who comes into the West to labor and to share the vicissitudes of new settlements; not the adventurer, who would repine at toil, and gather where he has not sown.

As I have looked abroad upon the vast domain of the West beyond the dim Missouri, or in the immediate valley of the Mississippi, I have wondered at the contrast presented between the comparatively small number who penetrate to the frontier, and that great throng of men who toil hard for a temporary livelihood in the populous towns and cities of the Union. And I have thought if this latter class were at all mindful of the opportunities for gain and independence which the new territories afforded, they would soon abandon— in a great measure at least— their crowded alleys in the city, and aspire to be cultivators and owners of the soil. Why there has not been a greater emigration from cities I cannot imagine, unless it is owing to a misapprehension of Western life. Either it is this, or the pioneer is possessed of a very superior degree of energy.

It has been said that the frontier man always keeps on the frontier; that he continues to emigrate as fast as the country around him becomes settled. There is a class that do so. Not, however, for the cause which has been sometimes humorously assigned— that civilization was inconvenient to them— but because good opportunities arise to dispose of the farms they have already improved; and because a further emigration secures them cheaper lands. The story of the pioneer who was disturbed by society, when his nearest neighbor lived fifteen miles off, even if it be true, fails to give the correct reason for the migratory life of this class of men.

It almost always happens that wherever we go somebody else has preceded us. Accident or enterprise has led some one to surpass us. Many of the most useful pioneers of this country have been attracted hither by the accounts given of its advantages by some one of their friends who had previously located himself here. Ask a man why he comes, and he says a neighbor of his, or a son, or a brother, has been in the territory for so many months, and he likes it so well I concluded to come also. A very respectable gentleman from Maine, a shipowner and a man of wealth, who came up on the boat with me to St. Paul, said his son-in-law was in the territory, and he had another son at home who was bound to come, and if his wife was willing he believed the whole family would come. Indeed the excellent state of society in the territory is to be attributed very much to the fact that parents have followed after their children.

It is pretty obvious too why men will leave poor farms in New England, and good farms in Ohio, to try their fortunes here. The farmer in New England, it may be in New Hampshire, hears that the soil of Minnesota is rich and free from rocks, that there are other favorable resources, and a salubrious climate such as he has been accustomed to. He concludes that it is best to sell out the place he has, and try ploughing where there are no rocks to obstruct him. The farmer of Ohio does not expect to find better soil than he leaves; but his inducements are that he can sell his land at forty or fifty dollars an acre, and preempt as good in Minnesota for a dollar and a quarter an acre. This operation leaves him a surplus fund, and he becomes a more opulent man, with better means to adorn his farm and to educate his children.

Those who contemplate coming West to engage in agricultural employment should leave their families, if families they have, behind till they have selected a location and erected some kind of a habitation; provided, however, they have no particular friend whose hospitality they can avail themselves of till their preliminary arrangements are effected. It will require three months, I judge, for a man to select a good claim (a quarter section, being 160 acres), and fence and plough a part of it and to erect thereon a cabin. There is never a want of land to preempt in a new country. The settler can always get an original claim, or buy out the claim of another very cheap, near some other settlers. The liberal policy of our government in regard to the disposal of public lands is peculiarly beneficial to the settler. The latter has the first chance. He can go on to a quarter section which may be worth fifteen dollars an acre, and preempt it before it is surveyed, and finally obtain it for $1.25 an acre. Whereas the speculator must wait till the land is surveyed and advertised for sale; and then he can get only what has not been preempted, and at a price which it brings at auction, not less than $1.25 an acre. Then what land is not sold at public sale is open to private entry at $1.25 an acre. It is such land that bounty warrants are located on. Thus it is seen the pioneer has the first choice. Why, I have walked over land up here that would now bring from ten to twenty dollars an acre if it was in the market, and which any settler can preempt and get for $1.25 an acre. I am strongly tempted to turn farmer myself, and go out and build me a cabin. The speculation would be a good one. But to acquire a title by preemption I must dwell on the soil, and prove that I have erected a dwelling and made other improvements. In other words, before a man (or any head of a family) can get a patent, he must satisfy the land officers that he is a dweller in good faith on the soil. It is often the case, indeed, that men get a title by preemption who never intend to live on their quarter section. But they do it by fraud. They have a sort of mental reservation, I suppose, when they take the requisite oaths. In this way many valuable claims are taken up and held along from month to month, or from year to year, by mock improvements. A pretender will make just improvements enough to hinder the actual settler from locating on the claim, or will sell out to him at a good profit. A good deal of money is made by these fictitious claimants. It is rather hard to prevent it, too, inasmuch as it is difficult to disprove that a man intends some time to have a permanent home, or, in fact, that his claim is not his legal residence, though his usual abiding place is somewhere else. Nothing could be more delightful than for a party of young men who desire to farm to come out together early in the spring, and aid each other in preempting land in the same neighborhood. The preemptor has to pay about five dollars in the way of fees before he gets through the entire process of securing a title. It is a popular error (much like the opinion that a man cannot swear to what he sees through glass) that improvements of a certain value, say fifty dollars, are required to be made, or that a certain number of acres must be cultivated. All that is required, however, is evidence that the party has built a house fit to live in, and has in good faith proceeded to cultivate the soil. The law does not permit a person to preempt 160 acres but once; yet this provision is often disregarded, possibly from ignorance, I was about to say, but that cannot be, since the applicant must make oath that he has not before availed himself of the right of preemption.

I will insert at this place an abridgment of the preemption act of 4th September, 1841, which I made two years ago; and which was extensively published in the new states and territories. I am happy to find, also, that it has been thought worth copying into one or more works on the West.

I. *Lands subject to preemption.* By sec. 10 of said act it is provided that the public lands to which the Indian title had been extinguished at the time of the settlement, and which had also been *surveyed* prior thereto, shall be subject to preemption, and purchase at the rate of one dollar and twenty-five cents per acre. And by the act of 22d July, 1854, sec. 12, the preemption of *unsurveyed* lands is recognised as legal. Lands of the following description are excepted: such as are included in any reservation, by any treaty, law, or proclamation of the President of the United States, or reserved for salines or for other purposes; lands included within the limits of any incorporated town, or which have been selected as the site for a city or town; lands actually settled and occupied for the purposes of trade and not agriculture; and lands on which are situated any known salines or mines.

II. *The amount* designated is any number of acres not exceeding one hundred and sixty.

III. *Who may preempt.* "Every person being the head of a family, or widow, or single man over the age of twenty-one years, and being a citizen of the United States, or having filed his declaration of intention to become a citizen, as required by the naturalization laws." But no person shall be entitled to more than one preemptive right, and no person who is the proprietor of three hundred and twenty acres of land in any state or territory of the United States, and no person who shall quit or abandon his residence on his own land to reside on the public land in the same state or territory, shall acquire any right of preemption.

IV. *The method to perfect the right.* The preemptor must make a settlement on the land in person; inhabit and improve the same, and erect thereon a dwelling. And when the land has been surveyed previous to settlement the preemptor shall, within thirty days of the date of the settlement, file with the register of the proper district a written statement describing the land settled upon, and declaring the intention of such person to claim the same under the provisions of the preemption law. And within twelve months of the date of the settlement such person shall make the requisite proof, affidavit, and payment. When unsurveyed lands are prompted (act of 1854), notice of the specific tracts claimed shall be filed with the surveyor general, within three months after the survey has been made in the field. And when two or more persons shall have settled on the same quarter section, the right of preemption shall be in him or her who made the first settlement; and questions arising between different settlers shall be decided by the register and receiver of the district within which the land is situated, subject to an appeal to and revision by the Secretary of the Interior of the United States.

And the settler must make oath before the receiver or register that he or she has never had the benefit of any right of preemption under the preemption act: that he or she is not the owner of three hundred and twenty acres of land in any state or territory of the United States, nor hath he or she settled upon and improved said land to sell the same on speculation, but in good faith to appropriate it to his or her own exclusive use or benefit: and that he or she has not directly or indirectly made any agreement or contract in any way or manner with any person or persons whatsoever, by which the title which he or she might acquire from the government of the United States should enure in whole or in part to the benefit of any person except himself or herself; and if any person talking such oath shall swear falsely in the premises, he or she shall be subject to all the pains and penalties of perjury, and shall forfeit the money which he or she may have paid for such land, and all right and title to the same; and any grant or conveyance which he or she may have made, except in the hands of bona fide purchasers for a valuable consideration, shall be null and void.

Proof of the requisite settlement and improvement shall be made by the preemptor to the satisfaction of the register and receiver, in the district in which the lands so claimed lie, who shall each be entitled to receive fifty cents from each applicant for his services rendered. as aforesaid; and all assignments and transfers of the right hereby secured prior to the issuing of the patent, shall be null and void. (See U. S. Stat. at Large, vol. 5, 453-458.)

But I was on the point of advising the settler what he should bring with him into a new country and what leave behind. He should not bring much furniture. It is very expensive and troublesome to have it transported. Nor will he need much to begin with, or have room for it. It will cost nearly as much to transport it seventy miles through the territory as it will to bring it from whence he started within the limits of the territory. Let him pack up in a small compass the most precious part of his inanimate household, and leave it ready for an agent to start it after he shall have found a domicil. This will save expensive storage. Then let his goods be directed to the care of some responsible forwarding merchant in a river town nearest to their final destination, that they may be taken care of and not be left exposed on the levee when they arrive. St.

Paul is now a place of so much mercantile importance and competition that one may buy provisions, furniture, or agricultural tools cheaper there than he can himself bring them from the East. The professional man, however, will do well to bring his books with him.

Let us assume now that the settler has got his house up, either a frame house or of logs, with a part of his farm fenced; and that be has filed his application for preemption at the land office in the district in which he resides. Let us suppose further, that he is passing his first autumn here. His house, if he is a man of limited means, has but two rooms, and they are both on the basement story. He has just shelter enough for his stock, but none for his hay, which is stacked near by. The probability is, that he lives in the vicinity of some clear stream or copious spring, and has not, therefore, needed to dig a well. The whole establishment, one would think, who was accustomed to the Eastern style of living, betrayed downright poverty.

But let us stop a moment; this is the home of a pioneer. He has been industrious, and everything about him exhibits forethought. There is a cornfield all fenced in with tamarack poles. It is paved over with pumpkins (for pumpkins flourish wonderfully in Minnesota), and contains twenty acres of ripe corn, which, allowing thirty-five bushels to an acre, is worth at ninety cents per bushel the sum of $630. There are three acres of potatoes, of the very best quality, containing three hundred bushels, which, at fifty cents a bushel, are worth $150. Here then, off of two crops, he gets $780, and I make a moderate estimate at that. Next year he will add to this a crop of oats or wheat. The true pioneer is a model farmer. He lays out his work two weeks in advance. Every evening finds him further ahead. If there is a rainy day, he knows what to set himself about. Be lays his plans in a systematic manner, and carries them into execution with energy. He is a true pioneer, and therefore he is not an idle man, nor a loafer, nor a weak addle-headed tippler. Go into his house, and though you do not see elegance you can yet behold intelligence, and neatness, and sweet domestic bliss. The life of the pioneer is not exposed to such hardships and delays as retarded the fortunes of the settlers in the older states. They had to clear forests; here the land is ready for the plough. And though "there is society where none intrude," yet he is not by any means beyond the boundaries of good neighborhood. In many cases, however, he has left his dearest friends far away in his native village, where his affections still linger. He has to endure painful separations, and to forego those many comforts which spring from frequent meetings under the parental roof, and frequent converse with the most attractive scenes of youth. But to compensate for these things he can feel that the labor of the pioneer, aside from its pecuniary advantage to himself, is of service to the state, and a helpmate to succeeding generations.

> "There are, who, distant from their native soil,
>   Still for their own and country's glory toil:
>   While some, fast rooted to their parent spot,
>   In life are useless, and in death forgot!"

LETTER XII.

SPECULATION AND BUSINESS.

Opportunities to select farms— Otter Tail Lake— Advantages of the actual settler over the speculator— Policy of new states as to taxing non-residents— Opportunities to make money— Anecdote of Col. Perkins— Mercantile business— Price of money— Intemperance— Education— The free school.

CROW WING, October, 1856.

IT is maintained by the reviewers, I believe, that the duller a writer is, the more accurate he should be. In the outset of this letter, I desire to testify my acquiescence in the justice of that dogma, for if, like neighbor Dogberry, "I were as tedious as a king," I could not find it in my heart to bestow it all without a measure of utility.

I shall try to answer some questions which I imagine might be put by different classes of men who are interested in this part of the west. My last letter had some hints to the farmer, and I can only add, in addition, for his benefit, that the most available locations are now a considerable distance above St. Paul. The valley of the St. Peter's is pretty much taken up; and so of the valley of the Mississippi for a distance of fifteen miles on either side to a point a hundred miles above St. Paul. One of the land officers at Minneapolis informed me that there were good preemption claims to be had fifteen miles west, that being as far as the country was thickly settled. One of the finest regions now unoccupied, that I know of, not to except even the country on the Crow Wing River, is the land bordering on Otter Tail Lake. For forty miles all round that lake the land is splendid. More than a dozen disinterested eye-witnesses have described that region to me in the most glowing terms. In beauty, in fertility, and in the various collateral resources which make a farming country desirable, it is not surpassed. It lies south of the picturesque highlands or *hauteurs des terres,* and about midway between the sources of the Crow Wing and North Red Rivers. From this town the distance to it is sixty miles. The lake itself is forty miles long and five miles in width. The water is clear and deep, and abounds with white fish that are famous for their delicious flavor. The following description, which I take from Captain Pope's official narrative of his exploration, is a reliable description of this delightful spot, now fortunately on the eve of being settled— " To the west, north-west, and north-east, the whole country is heavily timbered with oak, elm, ash, maple, birch, bass, &c., &c. Of these the sugar maple is probably the most valuable, and in the vicinity of Otter Tail Lake large quantities of maple sugar are manufactured by the Indians. The wild rice, which exists in these lakes in the most lavish profusion, constitutes a most necessary article of food with the Indians, and is gathered in large quantities in the months of September and October. To the east the banks of the lake are fringed with heavy oak and elm timber to the width of one mile. The whole region of country for fifty miles in all directions around this lake is among the most beautiful and fertile in the world. The fine scenery of lakes and open groves of oak timber, of winding streams connecting them, and beautifully rolling country on all sides, renders this portion of Minnesota the garden spot of the north-west. It is impossible in a report of this character to describe the feeling of admiration and astonishment with which we first beheld the charming country in the vicinity of this lake; and were I to give expression to my own feelings and opinions in reference to it, I fear they would be considered the ravings of a visionary or an enthusiast."[1] But let me say to the speculator that he need not covet any of these broad acres. There is little chance for him. Before that land can be bought at public sale or by mere purchasers at private sale, it will, I feel sure, be entirely occupied by actual settlers. And so it ought to be. The good of the territory is promoted by that beneficent policy of our public land laws which gives the actual settler the first and best chance to acquire a title by preemption.

[1 To illustrate the rapid progress which is going on constantly, I would remark that in less than a month after leaving Crow Wing, I received a letter from there informing me that Messrs. Crittenden, Cathcart, and others had been to Otter Tail Lake and laid out a town which they call Otter Tail City. The standing and means of the men engaged in the enterprise, are a sure guaranty of its success.]

Speculators have located a great many land warrants in Minnesota. Some have been located on lakes, some on swamps, some on excellent land. Of course the owner, who, as a general thing, is a nonresident, leaves his land idle for something to "turn up" to make it profitable. There it stands doing no good, but on the contrary is an encumbrance to the settler, who has to travel over and beyond it without meeting the face of a neighbor in its vicinity. The policy of new states is to tax non-resident landholders at a high rate. When the territory becomes a state, and is obliged to raise a revenue, some of these fellows outside, who, to use a phrase common up here, have plastered the country over with land warrants, will have to keep a lookout for the tax-gatherer. Now I do not mean to discourage moneyed men from investing in Minnesota lands. I do not wish to raise any bugbears, but simply to let them know that hoarding up large tracts of land without making improvements, and leaving it to increase in value by the toil and energy of the pioneer, is a way of doing things which is not popular with the actual settler. But there is a great deal of money to be made by judicious investments in land. Buying large tracts of land I believe to be the least profitable speculation, unless indeed the purchaser knows exactly what he is buying, and is on hand at the public sale to get the benefit of a second choice. I say second choice, because the preemptor has had the first choice long ago, and it may be before the land was surveyed. What I would recommend to speculators is to purchase in some good town sites. Buy in two or three, and if one or two happen to prove failures, the profits on the other will enable you to bear the loss. I know of a man who invested $6000 at St. Paul six years ago. He has sold over $80,000 worth of the land, and has as much more left. This is but an ordinary instance. The advantage of buying lots in a town arises from the rapid rise of the value of the land, the ready market, and withal the moderate prices at which they can be procured during the early part of its history.

To such persons as have a desire to come West, and are not inclined to be farmers, and who have not capital enough to engage in mercantile business, there is sufficient employment. A new country always opens avenues of successful business for every industrious man and woman; more kinds even than I could well enumerate. Every branch of mechanics needs workmen of all grades; from the boy who planes the rough boards to the head workman. Teaming affords good employment for young men the year round. The same may be said of the saw-mills. A great deal of building is going on constantly; and those who have good trades get $2.50 per day. I am speaking, of course, of the territory in general. One of the most profitable kinds of miscellaneous business is surveying. This art requires the services of large numbers; not only to survey the public lands, but town sites and the lands of private individuals. Labor is very high everywhere in the West, whether done by men, women, or children;— even the boys, not fourteen years old, who clean the knives and forks on the steamboats, get $20 a month and *are found*. But the best of it all is, that when a man earns a few dollars he can easily invest it in a piece of land, and double his money in three months, perhaps in one month. One of the merchant princes of Boston, the late Col. T. H. Perkins, published a notice in a Boston paper in 1789, he being then 25, that he would soon embark on board the ship Astrea for Canton, and that if any one desired to commit an "adventure" to him, they might be assured of his exertions for their interests. The practice of sending " adventures" "beyond the seas" is not so common as it was once; and instead thereof men invest their funds in western prizes. But let me remark in regard to the fact I relate, that it shows the true pioneer spirit. Col. Perkins was a pioneer. His energy led him beyond his counting-room, and he reaped the reward of his exertions in a great fortune.

I have now a young man in my mind who came to a town ten miles this side of St. Paul, six months ago, with $500. He commenced trading, and has already, by good investments and the profits of his business, doubled his money. Everything that one can eat or wear brings a high price, or as high as it does in any part of the West. The number of visitors and emigrants is so large that the productions of the territory are utterly inadequate to supply the market. Therefore large quantities of provisions have to be brought up the river from the lower towns. At Swan River, 100 miles this side of St. Paul, pork is worth $85. Knowing that pork constitutes a great part of the "victuals" up this way, though far from being partial to the article, I tried it when I dined at Swan River to see if it was good, and found it to be very excellent. Board for laboring men must be about four dollars a week. For transient guests at Crow Wing it is one dollar a day.

I have heard it said that money is scarce. It is possible. It certainly commands a high premium; but the reason is that there are such splendid opportunities to make fortunes by building and buying and selling city lots. A man intends that the rent of a house or store shall pay for its construction in three years. The profits of adventure justify a man in paying high interest. If a man has money enough to buy a pair of horses and a wagon, he can defy the world. These are illustrations to show why one is induced to pay interest. I do not think, however, money is "tight." I never saw people so free with their money, or appear to have it in so great abundance.

There is one drawback which this territory has in common with the greater part of the West, and in fact of the civilized world. It is not only a drawback, but a nuisance anywhere; I mean drinking or whiskey shops. The greater proportion of the settlers are temperate men, I am sure; but in almost every village there are places where the meanest kind of intoxicating liquor is sold. There are some who sell liquor to the Indians. But such business is universally considered as the most degraded that a mean man can be guilty of. It is filthy to see men staggering about under the influence of bad whiskey, or of any kind of whiskey. He who sends a young husband to his new cabin home intoxicated, to mortify and torment his family; or who sells liquor to the uneducated Indians, that they may fight and murder, must have his conscience— if he has any at all— cased over with sole leather. Mr. Gough is needed in the West.

Minnesota is not behind in education. Ever since Governor Slade, of Vermont, brought some bright young school mistresses up to St. Paul (in 1849), common school education has been diffusing its precious influences. The government wisely sets apart two sections of land— the 16th and 36th— in every township for school purposes. A township is six miles square; and the two sections thus reserved in each township comprise 1280 acres. Other territories have the same provision. This affords a very good fund for educational uses, or rather it is a great aid to the exertions of the people. There are some nourishing institutions of learning in the territory. But the greatest institution after all in the country— the surest protection of our liberties and our laws— is the FREE SCHOOL.

LETTER XIII.

CROW WING TO ST. CLOUD.

Pleasant drive in the stage— Scenery— The past— Fort Ripley Ferry— Delay at the Post Office— Belle Prairie— A Catholic priest— Dinner at Swan River— Potatoes— Arrival at Watab— St. Cloud.

ST. CLOUD, October, 1856.

YESTERDAY morning at seven I took my departure, on the stage, from Crow Wing. It was a most delightful morning, the air not damp, but bracing; and the welcome rays of the sun shed a mellow lustre upon a scene of "sylvan beauty." The first hour's ride was over a road I had passed in the dark on my upward journey, and this was the first view I had of the country immediately below Crow Wing. No settlements were to be seen, because the regulations of military reservations preclude their being made except for some purpose connected with the public interests. A heavy shower the night before had effectually laid the dust, and we bounded along on the easy coach in high spirits. The view of the prairie stretching "in airy undulations far away," and of the eddying current of the Mississippi, there as everywhere deep and majestic, with its banks skirted with autumn-colored foliage, was enough to commend the old fashioned system of stages to more general use. Call it poetry or what you please, yet the man who can contemplate with indifference the wonderful profusion of nature, undeveloped by art— inviting, yet never touched by the plough— must lack some one of the senses. Indeed, this picture, so characteristic of the new lands of the West, seems to call into existence a new sense. The view takes in a broad expanse which has never produced a stock of grain; and which has been traversed for ages past by a race whose greatest and most frequent calamity was hunger. If we turn to its past there is no object to call back our thoughts. All is oblivion. There are no ruins to awaken curious images of former life— no vestige of humanity— nothing but the present generation of nature. And yet there are traces of the past generations of nature to be seen. The depressions of the soil here and there to be observed, covered with a thick meadow grass, are unmistakeable indications of lakes which have now "vanished into thin air." That these gentle hollows were once filled with water is the more certain from the appearance of the shores of the present lakes, where the low water mark seems to have grown lower and lower every year. But if the past is blank, these scenes are suggestive of happy reflections as to the future. The long perspective is radiant with busy life and cheerful husbandry. New forms spring into being. Villages and towns spring up as if by magic, along whose streets throngs of men are passing. And thus, as "coming events cast their shadows before," does the mind wander from the real to the probable. An hour and a half of this sort of revery, and we had come to the Fort Ripley ferry, over which we were to go for the mail. That ferry (and I have seen others on the river like it) is a marvellous invention. It is a flat-boat which is quickly propelled either way across the river by means of the resistance which il offers to the current. Its machinery is so simple I will try to describe it. In the first place a rope is stretched across the river from elevated objects on either side. Each end of the boat is made fast to this line by pullies, which can be taken up or let out at the fastenings on the boat. All that is required to start the boat is to bring the bow, by means of the pully, to an acute angle with the current. The after part of the boat presents the principal resistance to the current by sliding a thick board into the water from the upper side. As the water strikes against this, the boat is constantly attempting to describe a circle, which it is of course prevented from doing by the current, and so keeps on— for it must move somewhere— in a direction where the obstruction is less. It certainly belongs to the science of hydraulics, for it is not such a boat as can be propelled by steam or wind. I had occasion recently to cross the Mississippi on a similar ferry, early in the morning, and before the ferryman was up. The proprietor of it was with me; yet neither of us knew much of its practical operation. I soon pulled the head of the boat towards the current, but left down the resistance board, or whatever it is called, at the bow as well as at the stern. This, of course, impeded our progress; but we got over in a few minutes; and I felt so much interested in this new kind of navigation, that I would have been glad to try the voyage over again.

On arriving within the square of the garrison, I expected to find the mail ready for delivery to the driver; but we had to wait half an hour. The mail is only weekly, and there was nothing of any consequence to change. We repaired to the post office, which was in a remote corner of a store-room, where the postmaster was busy making up his mail. Some of the officers had come in with documents which they wished to have mailed. And while we stood waiting, corporals and privates, servants of other officers brought in letters which Lieutenant So-and-so "was particularly desirous of having mailed this morning." The driver was magnanimous enough to submit to me whether we should wait. We all felt accommodating— the postmaster I saw was particularly so— and we concluded to wait till everything was in, and perhaps we would have waited for some one to write a letter. I could not but think it would be a week before another mail day; and still I could not but think these unnecessary morning hindrances were throwing a part of our journey into the night hours. Returning again to the eastern bank of the river by our fine ferry, we soon passed the spacious residence of Mr. Olmsted, a prominent citizen of the territory. We made a formal halt at his door to see if there were any passengers. Mr. Olmsted has a large farm under good cultivation, and several intelligent young men in his service. In that neighborhood are some other as handsome farms as I ever saw; but I think they are on the reservation, and are cultivated under the patronage of the war department. The winter grain was just up, and its fresh verdure afforded an agreeable contrast with the many emblems of decaying nature. It was in the middle of the forenoon that we reached Belle Prairie, along which are many good farm houses occupied by half-breeds. There is a church and a school-house. In the cemetery is a large cross painted black and white, and from its imposing appearance it cannot fail to make a solemn impression on minds which revere any tangible object that is consigned sacred. A very comfortable-looking house was pointed out to me as the residence of a Catholic priest, who has lived for many years in that section, spreading among the ignorant a knowledge of Christianity, and ministering to their wants in the hour of death. And though I am no Catholic, I could not but regard the superiority of that kind of preaching— for visiting the sick, consoling the afflicted, and rebuking sin by daily admonitions, is the true preaching of the Gospel— over the pompous declamation which now too often usurps the pulpit.

The dinner was smoking hot on the table when we drove up to the hotel at Swan River; and so charming a drive in the pure air had given me a keen appetite. The dinner (and I speak of these matters because they are quite important to travellers) was in all respects worthy of the appetite. The great staple article of Minnesota soil appears to be potatoes, for they were never known to be better anywhere else— Eastport not excepted— and at our table d'hote they were a grand collateral to the beef and pork. The dessert consisted of nice home made apple pies served with generosity, and we had tea or milk or water, as requested, for a beverage. After partaking of a dinner of this kind, the rest of the day's journey was looked forward to with no unpleasant emotions. The stage happened to be lightly loaded, and we rolled along with steady pace, and amidst jovial talk, till we reached the thriving, but to me not attractive, town of Watab. Three houses had been put up within the short time since I had stopped there. We got into Mr. Gilman's tavern at sundown. I was rejoiced to find a horse and carriage waiting for me, which had been kindly sent by a friend to bring me to St. Cloud. It is seven miles from Watab to this town. It was a charming moonlight evening, and I immediately started on with the faithful youth who had charge of the carriage, to enjoy my supper and lodging under the roof of my hospitable friend at St. Cloud.

LETTER XIV.

ST. CLOUD.— THE PACIFIC TRAIL.

Agreeable visit at St. Cloud— Description of the place— Causes of the rapid growth of towns— Gen. Lowry— The back country— Gov. Stevens's report— Mr. Lambert's views— Interesting account of Mr. A. W. Tinkham's exploration.

ST. CLOUD, October, 1856.

IF I follow the injunction of that most impartial and worthy critic, Lord Jeffrey, which is, that tourists should describe those things which make the pleasantest impression on their own minds, I should begin with an account of the delightful entertainment which genuine hospitality and courtesy have here favored me with. I passed Blannerhasset's Island once, and from a view of the scenery, sought something of that inspiration which, from reading Wirt's glowing description of it, I thought would be excited; but the reality was far below my anticipation. If applied to the banks of the Mississippi River, however, at this place, where the Sauk Rapids terminate, that charming description would be no more than an adequate picture. The residence of my friend is a little above the limits of St. Cloud, midway on the gradual rise from the river to the prairie. It is a neat white two-story cottage, with a piazza in front. The yard extends to the water's edge, and in it is a grove of handsome shade trees. Now that the leaves have fallen, we can sit on the piazza and have a full view of the river through the branches of the trees. The river is here very clear and swift, with a hard bottom; and if it were unadorned with its cheerful foliage-covered banks, the view of it would still add a charm to a residence. There is a mild tranquillity, blended with the romance of the scene, admirably calculated to raise in the mind emotions the most agreeable and serene. For nature is a great instructor and purifier. As Talfourd says in that charming little volume of Vacation Rambles, "to commune with nature and grow familiar with all her aspects, surely softens the manners as much, at the least, as the study of the liberal arts."

St. Cloud is favorably located on the west bank of the river, seventy-five miles above St. Paul. It is just enough elevated to have good drainage facilities, should it become densely populous. For many years it was the seat of a trading post among the Winnebagoes. But the date of its start as a town is not more than six months ago; since when it has been advancing with unsurpassed thrift, on a scale of affluence and durability. Its main street is surely a street in other respects than in the name; for it has on either side several neatly built three-story blocks of stores, around which the gathering of teams and of people denotes such an activity of business as to dispel any idea that the place is got up under false pretences. The St. Cloud advertisements in the St. Paul daily papers contain the cards of about forty different firms or individuals, which is a sort of index to the business of the place. A printing press is already in the town, and a paper will in a few days be issued. There are now two hotels; one of which (the Stearns House), it is said, cost $9000. A flourishing saw-mill was destroyed by fire, and in a few weeks another one was built in its place. An Episcopal church is being erected. The steamer "H. M. Rice" runs between here and St. Anthony. It is sometimes said that this is the head of the Upper Mississippi navigation, but such is not the case. The Sauk Rapids which terminate here are an obstruction to continuous navigation between St. Anthony and Crow Wing, but after you get to the latter place (where the river is twenty feet deep) there is good navigation for two hundred miles. There are several roads laid out to intersect at St. Cloud, for the construction of which, I believe, the government has made some appropriation. Town lots are sold on reasonable terms to those who intend to make improvements on them, which is the true policy for any town, but the general market price ranges from $100 to $1000 a lot. The town is not in the hands of capitalists, though moneyed men are interested in it. General Lowry is a large proprietor. He lives at Arcadia, just above the town limits, and has a farm consisting of three hundred acres of the most splendid land, which is well stocked with cattle and durably fenced. A better barn, or a neater farmyard than he has, cannot be found between Boston and Worcester. And while speaking of barns I would observe that the old New England custom of having good barns is better observed in Minnesota than anywhere else in the West. General Lowry has been engaged in mercantile business. He was formerly a member of the territorial council, and is a very useful and valuable citizen of the territory.

It would not be more surprising to have Eastern people doubt some of the statements concerning the growth of Western towns, than it was for the king of Siam to doubt that there was any part of the world where water changed from liquid to a hard substance. His majesty knew nothing about ice. Now, there are a good many handsome villages in the East which hardly support one store. Not that people in such a village do not consume as much or live in finer style; but the reason is that they are old settlers who produce very much that they live on, and who, by great travelling facilities, are able to scatter their trading custom into some commercial metropolis. Suppose, however, one of your large villages to be so newly settled that the people have had no chance to raise anything from their gardens or their fields, and are obliged to buy all they are to eat and all that is to furnish their dwellings, or equip their shops, or stock their farms; then you have a state of things which will support several stores, and a whole catalogue of trades. It is a state of affairs which corresponds with every new settlement in the West; or, indeed, which faintly compares with the demand for everything merchantable, peculiar in such places. Then again, besides the actual residents in a new place, who have money enough in their pockets, but nothing in their cellars, there is generally a large population in the back country of farmers and no stores. Such people come to a place like this to trade, for fifteen or twenty miles back, perhaps; and it being a county seat they have other objects to bring them. At the same time there is an almost constant flow of settlers through the place into the unoccupied country to find preemption claims, who, of course, wish to take supplies with them. The settler takes a day, perhaps, for his visit in town to trade. Time is precious with him, and he cannot come often. So he buys, perhaps, fifty or a hundred dollars worth of goods. These are circumstances which account for activity of business in these river towns, and which, though they are strikingly apparent here, are not peculiar to this town. At first, I confess, it was a mystery to me what could produce such startling and profitable trade in these new towns.

It was in the immediate vicinity of St. Cloud that Gov. Stevens left the Mississippi on his exploration, in 1853, of a railroad route to the

Pacific. Several crossings of the river had been previously examined, and it was found that one of the favorable points for a railroad bridge over it was here. I might here say that the country directly west lies in the valley of Sauk River, and from my own observation I know it to be a good farming country; and I believe the land is taken up by settlers as far back as twelve miles. It is a little upwards of a hundred miles in a westerly direction from St. Cloud to where the expedition first touched the Bois des Sioux (or Sioux Wood River). Gov. Stevens says in his report— " The plateau of the Bois des Sioux will be a great centre of population and communication. It connects with the valley of the Red River of the North, navigable four hundred miles for steamers of three or four feet draught, with forty-five thousand square miles of arable and timber land; and with the valley of the Minnesota, also navigable at all seasons when not obstructed by ice, one hundred miles for steamers, and occasionally a hundred miles further. The head of navigation of the Red River of the North is within one hundred and ten miles of the navigable portion of the Mississippi, and is distant only forty miles from the Minnesota. Eastward from these valleys to the great lakes, the country on both sides of the Mississippi is rich, and much of it heavily timbered."

I will also add another remark which he makes, inasmuch as the character of the country in this latitude, as far as the Pacific shore, must have great influence on this locality; and it is this: " Probably four thousand square miles of tillable land is to be found immediately on the eastern slopes of (the Rocky Mountains); and at the bottoms of the different streams, retaining their fertility for some distance after leaving the mountains, will considerably increase this amount." Mr. John Lambert, the topographer of the exploration, divides the country between the Mississippi and Columbia rivers, into three grand divisions. The first includes the vast prairies between the Mississippi and the base of the Rocky Mountains. The second is the mountain division, embracing about five degrees of longitude. The third division comprises the immense plains of the Columbia.

Of the first division— from here to the foot of the Rocky Mountains— let me quote what Mr. Lambert in his official report calls a "passing glance." "Undulating and level prairies, skirted with woods of various growth, and clothed everywhere with a rich verdure; frequent and rapid streams, with innumerable small but limpid lakes, frequented by multitudes of waterfowl, most conspicuous among which appears the stately swan; these, in ever-recurring succession, make up the panorama of this extensive district, which may be said to be everywhere fertile, beautiful, and inviting. The most remarkable features of this region are the intervals of level prairie, especially that near the bend of Red River, where the horizon is as unbroken as that of a calm sea. Nor are other points of resemblance wanting— the long grass, which in such places is unusually rank, bending gracefully to the passing breeze as it sweeps along the plain, gives the idea of waves (as indeed they are); and the solitary horseman on the horizon is so indistinctly seen as to complete the picture by the suggestion of a sail, raising the first feeling of novelty to a character of wonder and delight. The following outlines of the rolling prairies are broken only by the small lakes and patches of timber which relieve them of monotony and enhance their beauty; and though marshes and sloughs occur, they are of too small extent and too infrequent to affect the generally attractive character of the country. The elevation of the rolling prairies is generally so uniform, that even the summits between streams flowing in opposite directions exhibit no peculiar features to distinguish them from the ordinary character of the valley slopes."

I think I cannot do a better service to the emigrant or settler than to quote a part of the report made by Mr. A. W. Tinkham, descriptive of his route from St. Paul to Fort Union. His exploration, under Gov. Stevens, was made in the summer of 1853; and he has evidently given an impartial account of the country. I begin with it where he crosses the Mississippi in the vicinity of St. Cloud. The part quoted embraces the route for a distance of two hundred and ninety-five miles; the first seventy miles of which was due west— the rest of the route being a little north of west.

"*June* 9. Ferried across the Mississippi River, here some six hundred to eight hundred feet wide— boating the camp equipage, provisions, &c., and swimming the animals; through rich and fertile prairies, variegated with the wooded banks of Sauk River, a short distance on the left, with the wooded hills on either side, the clustered growth of elm, poplar, and oak, which the road occasionally touches; following the 'Red River trail,' we camp at Cold Spring Brook, with clear, cool water, good grass, and wood.

"*June* 10. Cold Spring Brook is a small brook about ten feet across, flowing through a miry slough, which is very soft and deep, and previous to the passage of the wagons, had, for about two hundred feet distance, been bridged in advance by a causeway of round or split logs of the poplar growth near by; between this and the crossing of Sauk River are two other bad sloughs, over one of which are laid logs of poplar, and over the other the wagons were hauled by hand, after first removing the loads. Sauk River is crossed obliquely with a length of ford some three hundred feet— depth of water four-and-a-half to five feet; goods must be boated or rafted over, the river woods affording the means of building a raft; camped immediately after crossing; wood, water, and grass good and abundant.

"*June* 11. Over rolling prairies, without wood on the trail, although generally in sight on the right or left, with occasional small ponds and several bad sloughs, across which the wagons were hauled over by hand to Lake Henry— a handsome, wooded lake; good wood and grass; water from small pond; not very good.

"*June* 13. Passing over rolling prairies to a branch of Crow River, the channel of which is only some twenty feet wide and four or five feet deep; but the water makes back into the grass one hundred feet or more from the channel as early in the season as when crossed by the train. Goods boated over; wagons by hand and with ropes; no wood on the stream; several small lakes, not wooded, are on either side of the trail, with many ducks, geese, and plovers on them: encamp at Lightning Lake, a small and pretty lake, sufficiently well wooded on the borders for camping purposes; good water, wood, and grass, and abounding with fish.

"*June* 18. Over rolling prairie with small pools and marshes, to a swift running stream about twenty feet wide, three feet deep, a branch of Chippewa River; heavily rolling ground with stony knolls and granite boulders, to White Bear Lake, a large handsome lake, with mingled open and woodland.

"Broken rolling ground to camp, a mile off the Red River trail, and near a small wooded lake. Two small brooks have to be crossed in the interval, and being somewhat deep and with abrupt sides, are troublesome crossings.

"*June* 20. Rolling prairie country, with small marshes and ponds to a tributary of South Branch. Swift running stream, gravelly bottom, fifteen feet wide, three to four feet deep; with care in selection good crossing was obtained for the wagons; a wooded lake is a short distance to the right of trail.

"Small rivulet, whose banks are marshy and soft.

"Prairies, with small marshes and ponds to a swift running brook, six feet wide.

"Prairie to Pike Lake and camp of St. Grover; a handsome lake of about a mile in diameter, said to abound in pike; well wooded on its south border; grass, water, and wood, for camping, abundant and good.

"Rolling prairie with knolls; several ponds and marshes, with an intervening brook about six feet wide, and rather difficult of passage, from the abruptness of its banks, to a small brook, the outlet of a small and partially wooded lake or pond.

"Rolling prairie, with grassy, swelling knolls, small ponds and marshes, to Chippeway River; camp of odometer wagon on edge of river; water and grass good; no wood.

"*June* 24. Crossed Chippeway River, one hundred and twenty-four feet wide, three to six feet deep; goods boated over, and the animals swimming; wagon hauled through the water by a rope attached to the tongue, and with the aid of the mules; camped on Elk Lake, a small and pretty lake, well wooded, and with luxuriant grass; good water.

"*June* 25. Trail passes over prairies with a rich heavy grass (this is a hundred miles west of the Mississippi River), about eighteen inches high, winding between wooded lakes to a heavy ravine, with a small and sluggish rivulet in its bottom; sides steep, and laborious for the wagon train.

"Prairie sloping towards the western branch of the Chippeway River; a stream when crossed, about one hundred and forty feet wide, three or four feet deep, with a marked current and firm bottom; no wood.

"Camp on a small lake, fairly wooded, with luxuriant grass, and good water.

"*June* 27. Undulating prairie, rich soil, covered with a heavy growth of grass, with small ponds and marshes; woods continue in sight a short distance on the left of Elbow Lake, a well wooded lake, of form indicated by its name.

"Rolling prairie, with two bad sloughs, to Rabbit River, which is crossed with the wagon with but little difficulty, where it issues from a small lake. It is a small stream, but spreads out from one hundred to three hundred feet, with marshy borders; camp on the small lake, with good grass, wood, and water.

"*June* 28. Rolling ground, with small ponds and marshes, to a small brook twelve feet wide; the Bois des Sioux prairie, a smooth, flat prairie, without knoll or undulation— an immense plain, apparently level, covered with a tall, coarse, dark-colored grass, and unrelieved with the sight of a tree or shrub; firm bottom, but undoubtedly wet in spring; small brook, when the train made a noon halt.

"Same smooth prairie as above to Bois des Sioux River, sometimes soft and miry; camp on river bank; wood and grass good— river water fair; many catfish caught in the river.

"*June* 29. Cross Bois des Sioux River; seventy feet wide, four to seven feet deep; muddy bottom; steep and miry banks; goods boated over; wagons hauled through, light, with ropes; bad crossing, but passable; smooth flat prairie, as on the east side of Bois des Sioux, occasionally interrupted with open sloughs to Wild Rice River, and camp with wood, water, and abundant grass.

"*June* 30. Wild Rice River, about forty feet wide and five and a half feet deep, with muddy and miry bottom and sides, flowing in a canal-like channel, some twenty feet below prairie level; river skirted with elm— bridged from the steep banks, being too miry to sustain the animals, detaining the train but little more than half-a-day; small brook without wood, flowing in a broad channel cut out through the prairie; crossing miry, but made passable for the wagon by strewing the bottom with mown grass.

"Firm prairie to camp on edge of above small stream; good grass and water; no wood; elk killed by hunter.

"*July* 1. Smooth prairie extending to Shayenne River; sand knolls, ponds, and marshes frequent as the river is approached. The marshes were not miry— firmer bottom; good wagon road; night encampment on bank of river; sufficient grass for train; wood abundant; river water good; many catfish caught in river.

"*July* 2. Shayenne River, sixty feet wide, fourteen feet deep; river had been previously bridged by Red River train, from the poplars and other trees growing on the river, and this bridge we made use of in crossing our wagons; camp on the west bank of the river; water, wood, and grass good.

"*July* 4. Prairie undulation, interrupted with marshes, small ponds and occasional small rivulets, to Maple River, about twenty-five feet wide, three and a half feet deep, firm bottom, and easily passed by the wagons; river tolerably well wooded, and the camp on its edge is furnished with water, wood, and good grass. The rich black soil of the valley of this stream is noticeable.

"*July* 5. To a small stream thirty feet wide, two feet deep, clayey bottom, easily crossed by the wagons; prairie high, firm, and almost level for some thirteen miles, becoming more rolling and with small ponds in the last seven miles of the march; on the edge of some of the ponds are salt incrustations; camp on the river; water good; grass good; no wood, and the bois de vache is used for fuel.

"*July* 6. Country wet and marshy; not a tree in sight; prairie with low ridges and knolls, and great number of ponds and marshes; night's camp by a small pond; no wood, but plenty of bois de vache; grass good.

"*July* 7. Approaching the Shayenne; country as yesterday for some half dozen miles; bordering on the river the ground is broken with deep coulees and ravines, and to keep away from them the train kept at some distance from the river, encamping by a small marshy pond; no wood; plenty of bois de vache; grass good; water tolerable; first buffalo killed to-day.

"*July* 8. Prairie swelling with ridges; descend to the Shayenne, which flows some one hundred and fifty to two hundred feet below the prairie by a steep hill; camp in the bottom of the river; wood and water good; grass rather poor; the bottom of the Shayenne, some half a mile wide, is often soft and miry, but when crossed by the train firm and dry.

"*July* 9. Cross the Shayenne, fifty feet wide, three and a half feet deep; immediate banks some ten feet high, and requiring some digging to give passage to the wagons.

"Prairie with swelling ridges and occasional marshes to camp, to a slough affording water and grass; no wood; buffalo very abundant.

"*July* 10. Prairie swelling into ridges and hills, with a frequency of marshes, ponds, and sloughs; camp at a pretty lake, near Lake Jessie; fairly wooded, with water slightly saline; grass scanty, having been consumed by the buffalo. Prairies covered with buffalo."

I take this valuable sketch of the natural features of the country from volume 1 of Explorations and Surveys for the Pacific Railroad (page 353-356); for which I am indebted to the learned Secretary of War.

LETTER XV.

ST. CLOUD TO ST. PAUL.

Importance of starting early — Judge Story's theory of early rising — Rustic scenery — Horses and mules — Surveyors — Humboldt — Baked fish — Getting off the track — Burning of hay stacks — Supper at St. Anthony — Arrival at the Fuller House.

ST. PAUL, October, 1856.

I WAS up by the gray dawn of the morning of yesterday, and after an early but excellent breakfast, crossed the river from St. Cloud, in order to meet the stage at Sauk Rapids. As we came up on the main road, the sight of a freshly made rut, of stage-wheel size, caused rather a disquieting apprehension that the stage had passed.

But my nerves were soon quieted by the assurance from an early hunter, who was near by shooting prairie chickens while they were yet on the roost, that the stage had not yet come. So we kept on to the spacious store where the post office is kept; where I waited and waited for the stage to come which was to bring me to St. Paul. It did not arrive till eight o'clock. I thought if every one who had a part to perform in starting off the stage from Watab (for it had started out from there that morning), was obliged to make the entire journey of 80 miles to St. Paul in the stage, they would prefer to get up a little earlier rather than have the last part of the trip extended into "the dead waist and middle of the night." I remarked to the driver, who is a very clever young man, that the stage which left St. Paul started as early as five o'clock, and I could not see why it was not as necessary to start as early in going down, inasmuch as the earlier we started the less of the night darkness we had to travel in. He perfectly agreed with me, and attributed his inability to start earlier to the dilatory arrangements at the hotel. When jogging along at about eleven at night between St. Anthony and the city, I could not help begrudging every minute of fair daylight which had been wasted. The theory of Judge Story, that it don't make much difference when a man gets up in the morning, provided he is wide awake after he is up, will do very well, perhaps, except when one is to start on a journey in the stage.

I took a seat by the driver's side, the weather being clear and mild, and had an unobstructed and delightful view of every object, and there seemed to be none but pleasant objects in range of the great highway. Though there is, between every village, population enough to remind one constantly that he is in a settled country, the broad extent yet unoccupied proclaims that there is still room enough. Below Sauk Rapids a good deal of the land on the road side is in the hands of speculators. This, it is understood, is on the east side of the Mississippi. On the west side there are more settlements. But yet there are many farms, with tidy white cottages; and in some places are to be seen well-arranged flower-gardens. The most attractive scenery to me, however, was the ample corn-fields, which, set in a groundwork of interminable virgin soil, are pictures which best reflect the true destiny and usefulness of an agricultural region. We met numerous teams heavily laden with furniture or provisions, destined for the different settlements above. The teams are principally drawn by two horses; and, as the road is extremely level and smooth, are capable of taking on as much freight as under other circumstances could be drawn by four horses. Mules do not appear to be appreciated up this way so much as in Missouri or Kentucky. Nor was it unusual to meet light carriages with a gentleman and lady, who, from the luggage, &c., aboard, appeared to have been on somewhat of an extensive shopping expedition. And I might as well say here, if I havn't yet said it, that the Minnesotians are supplied with uncommonly good horses. I do not remember to have seen a mean horse in the territory. I suppose, as considerable pains are taken in raising stock, poor horses are not raised at all; and it will not pay to import poor ones. A company of surveyors whom we met excited a curiosity which I was not able to solve. It looked odd enough to see a dozen men walking by the side or behind a small one-horse cart; the latter containing some sort of baggage which was covered over, as it appeared, with camping fixtures. It was more questionable whether the team belonged to the men than that the men were connected with the team. The men were mostly young and very intelligent-looking, dressed with woollen shirts as if for out door service, and I almost guessed they were surveyors; yet still thought they were a party of newcomers who had concluded to club together to make their preemption claim. But surveyors they were.

The town of Humboldt is the county seat for Sherburne county. It lies between the Mississippi and Snake rivers. The part of the town which I saw was a very small part. Mr. Brown's residence, which is delightfully situated on the shore of a lake, is at once the court house and the post office, besides being the general emporium and magnate of Humboldt business and society. Furthermore, it is the place where the stage changes horses and where passengers on the down trip stop to dine. It was here we stopped to dine; and as the place had been a good deal applauded for its table-d'hote, a standard element of which was said to be baked fish, right out of the big lake, I at least had formed very luxurious expectations. Mr. Brown was away. We had met his lively countenance on his way up to a democratic caucus. Perhaps that accounted for our not having baked fish, for fish we certainly did not have. The dinner was substantial, however, and yielded to appetites which had been sharpened by a half day's inhalation of serene October air. We had all become infused with a spirit of despatch; and were all ready to start, and did start, in half an hour from the time we arrived at the house.

We had not proceeded far after dinner before meeting the Monticello stage, which runs between the thriving village of that name — on the west bank of the Mississippi — and St. Paul. It carries a daily mail. There were several passengers aboard.

One little incident in our afternoon travel I will mention, as it appeared to afford more pleasure to the rest of the passengers than it did to me. Where the stage was to stop for fifteen or twenty minutes, either to change mail or horses, I had invariably walked on a mile, if I could get as far, for the sake of variety and exercise. So when we came to the pretty village of Anoka (at the mouth of Rum River), where the mail was to be changed, I started on foot and alone. But unfortunately and unconsciously I took the wrong road. I had walked a mile I think — for twenty minutes at least had expired since I started — and being in the outskirts of the town, in the midst of farms and gardens, turned up to a garden-fence, on the other side of which a gentleman of professional — I rather thought clerical appearance — was feeding a cow on pumpkins. I had not seen pumpkins so abundant since my earliest youth, when I used to do a similar thing. I rather thought too that the gentleman whom I accosted was a Yankee, and after talking a few minutes with him, so much did he exceed me in asking questions, that I felt sure he was one. How thankful I ought to be that he was one! for otherwise it is probable he would not have ascertained where, and for what purpose, I was walking. He informed me I was on the wrong road; that the stage took a road further west, which was out of sight; and that I had better go on a little further and then cross the open prairie. Then for the first time did I notice that the road I had taken was but a street, not half so much worn as the main road. I followed his friendly advice, and feeling some despair I hastened on at a swift run, and as I advanced towards where I thought the right road ought to be, though I could neither see it nor the stage, "called so loud that all the hollow deep of" — the prairies might have resounded. At last, when quite out of breath and hoarse with loud vociferation, I descried the stage rolling on at a rapid rate. Then I renewed my calls, and brought it up standing. After clambering over a few fences, sweating and florid, I got to the stage and resumed my seat, amidst the pleasant merriment of the passengers. The driver was kind enough to say that he began to suspect I had taken the wrong road, and was about to turn round and come after me— that he certainly would not have left me behind, &c. I was happy, nevertheless, that my mistake did not retard the stage. But I do not intend to abandon the practice of walking on before the stage whenever it stops to change horses.

Just in the edge of twilight, and when we were a little way this side of Coon Creek, where we had changed horses again, we came in sight of a large fire. It was too much in one spot to be a prairie fire; and as we drove on the sad apprehension that it was a stack of hay was confirmed. The flames rose up in wide sheets, and cast a steady glare upon the landscape. It was a gorgeous yet a dismal sight. It always seems worse to see grain destroyed by fire than ordinary merchandise. Several stacks were burning. We saw that the usual precaution against prairie fires had been taken. These consist in ploughing several furrows around the stack, or by burning the grass around it to prevent the flames from reaching it. It was therefore suspected that some rascal had applied the torch to the hay; though for humanity's sake we hoped it was not so. The terrible prairie fires, which every autumn waste the western plains, are frequently started through the gross carelessness of people who camp out, and leave their fires burning.

Some of us took supper at St. Anthony. I cannot say much of the hotel *de facto*. The table was not as good as I found on the way at other places above. There is a hotel now being built there out of stone, which I am confident will exceed anything in the territory, if we except the Fuller House. It is possible we all felt invigorated and improved by the supper, for we rode the rest of the way in a very crowded stage without suffering any exhibition of ill temper to speak of, and got into St. Paul at last, when it was not far from eleven; and after seventy-five miles of staging, the luxurious accommodations of the Fuller House seemed more inviting than ever.

LETTER XVI.

PROGRESS.

Rapid growth of the North-West— Projected railroads— Territorial system of the United States— Inquiry into the cause of Western progress— Influence of just laws and institutions— Lord Bacon's remark.

ST. PAUL, October, 1856.

THE progress which has characterized the settlement of the territory of Minnesota, presents to the notice of the student of history and political economy some important facts. The growth of a frontier community, so orderly, so rapid, and having so much of the conservative element in it, has rarely been instanced in the annals of the world. In less time than it takes the government to build a custom house we see an unsettled territory grown to the size of a respectable state, in wealth, in population, in power. A territory, too, which ten years ago seemed to be an incredible distance from the civilized portions of the country; and which was thought by most people to be in a latitude that would defeat the energy and the toil of man. Today it could bring into the field a larger army than Washington took command of at the beginning of our revolution!

In 1849, the year of its organization, the population of the territory was 4780; now it is estimated to be nearly 200,000. In 1852 there were 42 post offices in the territory, now there are 253. The number of acres of public land sold during the fiscal year ending 30th June, 1852, was 15,258. For the year ending 30th June, 1856, the number of acres sold was 1,002,130.

When we contemplate the headlong progress of Western growth in its innumerable evidences of energy, we admit the truth of what the Roman poet said— *nil mortalibus ardum est*— that there is nothing too difficult for man. In the narrative of his exploration to the Mississippi in 1820, along with General Cass, Mr. Schoolcraft tells us how Chicago then appeared. "We found," says he, "*four or five families living here.*" Four or five families was the extent of the population of Chicago in 1820! In 1836 it had 4853 inhabitants. In 1855 its population was 85,000. The history of many western towns that have sprung up within ten years is characterized by much the same sort of thrift. Unless some terrible scourge shall come to desolate the land, or unless industry herself shall turn to sloth, a few more years will present the magnificent spectacle of the entire domain stretching from this frontier to the Pacific coast, transformed into a region of culture, "full of life and splendor and joy."

At present there are no railroads in operation in Minnesota; but those which are already projected indicate, as well as any statistics, the progress which is taking place. The Chicago, St. Paul, and Fond-du-Lac Railroad was commenced some two years ago at Chicago, and over 100 miles of it are completed. It is to run *via* Hudson in Wisconsin, Stillwater, St. Paul, and St. Anthony in Minnesota to the western boundary of the territory. Recently it has united with the Milwaukee and La Cross Road, which secures several millions of acres of valuable land, donated by congress, and which will enable the stockholders to complete the road to St. Paul and St. Anthony within two years. A road has been surveyed from the head of Lake Superior *via* St. Paul to the southern line of the territory, and will soon be worked. The Milwaukee and Mississippi Railroad Company will in a few weeks have their road completed to Prairie du Chien, and are extending it on the east side of the Mississippi to St. Paul. Another road is being built up the valley of the Red Cedar River in Iowa to Minneapolis. The Keokuck road is in operation over fifty miles, and will soon be under contract to St. Paul. This road is to run *via* the valley of the Des Moines River, through the rich coal fields of Iowa, and will supply the upper Mississippi and Lake Superior region with coal.

The Green Bay and Minnesota Railroad Company has been organized and the route selected. This road will soon be commenced. The active men engaged in the enterprise reside in Green Bay and Stillwater. A company has been formed and will soon commence a road from Winona to the western line of the territory. The St. Anthony and St. Paul Railroad Company will have their line under contract early the coming season. The Milwaukee and La Cross Company propose continuing their road west through the valley of Root River, through Minnesota to the Missouri River. Another company has been formed for building a road from the head of Lake

Superior to the Red River of the North.[1] Such are some of the railroad enterprises which are under way, and which will contribute at an early day to develop the opulent resources of the territory. A railroad through this part of the country to the Pacific is among the probable events of the present generation.

[1 The following highly instructive article on navigation, I take from The *Pioneer and Democrat* (St. Paul), of the 20th November:

"GROWTH OF THE STEAMBOATING BUSINESS— THE SEASON OF 1856.

— About ten years after the first successful attempt at steamboat navigation on the Ohio River, the first steamboat that ever ascended the Upper Mississippi River to Fort Snelling, arrived at that post. This was the 'Virginia,' a stern-wheel boat, which arrived at the Port in the early part of May, 1823. From 1823 to 1844 there were but few arrivals each year— sometimes not more than two or three. The steamers running on the Upper Mississippi, at that time, were used altogether to transport supplies for the Indian traders and the troops stationed at Fort Snelling. Previous to the arrival of the Virginia, keel boats were used for this purpose, and sixty days' time, from St. Louis to the Fort, was considered a good trip.

"By a reference to our files, we are enabled to present, at a glance, the astonishing increase in steamboating business since 1844. The first boat to arrive that year, was the Otter, commanded by Captain Harris. The following table presents the number of arrivals since that time:—

Year	First Boat	No. of Arrivals	River Closed
1844	April 6	41	Nov. 23
1845	April 6	48	Nov. 26
1846	March 31	24	Dec. 5
1847	April 7	47	Nov. 29

1848	April 7	63	Dec. 4
1849	April 9	85	Dec. 7
1850	April 9	104	Dec. 4
1851	April 4	119	Nov. 28
1852	April 16	171	Nov. 18
1853	April 11	200	Nov. 30
1854	April 8	245	Nov. 27
1855	April 17	560	Nov. 20
1856	April 18	837	Nov. 10

"In 1851, three boats went up the Minnesota River, and in 1852, one boat ran regularly up that stream during the season. In 1853, the business required an average of one boat per day. In 1854, the business had largely increased, and in 1855, the arrivals of steamers from the Minnesota, amounted to 119.

"The present season, on the Mississippi, has been a very prosperous one, and the arrivals at St. Paul exhibit a gratifying increase over any preceding year, notwithstanding the season of navigation has been two weeks shorter than last season. Owing to the unusually early gorge in the river at Hastings, upwards of fifty steamers bound for this port, and heavily laden with merchandise and produce, were compelled to discharge their cargoes at Hastings and Stillwater.

"Navigation this season opened on the 18th of April. The Lady Franklin arrived on the evening of that day from Galena. Previous to her arrival, there had been eighteen arrivals at our landing from the head of Lake Pepin, and twelve arrivals at the foot of the lake, from Galena and Dubuque.

"During the present season, seventy-eight different steamers have arrived at our wharf, from the points mentioned in the following table. This table we draw mainly from the books of the City Marshal, and by reference to our files.

FROM ST. LOUIS.	
Boats	*No. of Trips.*
Ben Coursin	19
A. G. Mason	8
Metropolitan	13
Audubon	5
Golden State	8
Laclede	11
Luella	8
Cheviot	1
James Lyon	7
Vienna	5
New York	1
Delegate	1
Mansfield	7
Forest Rose	1

Ben Bolt	2
J. P. Tweed	1
Fire Canoe	2
Carrier	1
Julia Dean	1
Resolute	2
Gossamer	4
Thomas Scott	6
Gipsey	2
W. G. Woodside	1
York State	5
Mattie Wayne	4
Brazil	4
Dan Convers	1
Henrietta	4
Editor	5
Minnesota Belle	8
Rochester	2

Oakland	7
Grace Darling	4
Montauk	3
Fairy Queen	1
Saint Louis	1
Americus	2
Atlanta	1
Jacob Traber	6
White Bluffs	1
Arcola	8
Conewago	10
Lucie May	8
Badger State	5
Sam Young	4
Violet	1

Total arrivals from St. Louis,	212

FROM FULTON CITY.

Falls City	11
Diamond	1
H. T. Yeatman	11
Time and Tide	5

Total from Fulton City,	28

FROM GALENA AND DUNLEITH.	
Lady Franklin	23
Galena	30
Alhambra	21
Royal Arch	6
Northern Belle	28
Banjo	1
War Eagle	17
City Belle	30
Golden Era	29
Ocean Wave	28
Granite State	12

Greek Slave	3

Total from Galena and Dunleith,	228

FROM DUBUQUE.	
Excelsior	23
Kate Cassel	29
Clarion	11
Tishimingo	3
Fanny Harris	28
Flora	29
Hamburg	12

Total from Dubuque,	135

FROM MINNESOTA RIVER.	
H. T. Yeatman	4
Globe	34
Clarion	12

Reveille	40
H. S. Allen	10
Time and Tide	11
Wave	29
Equator	46
Minnesota Valley	20
Berlin	10

Total from Minnesota River,	216

RECAPITULATION.		
Number of arrivals from	St. Louis	212
	Fulton City	28
	Galena and Dunleith	228
	Dubuque	135
	Minnesota River	216
	head of Lake Pepin	18

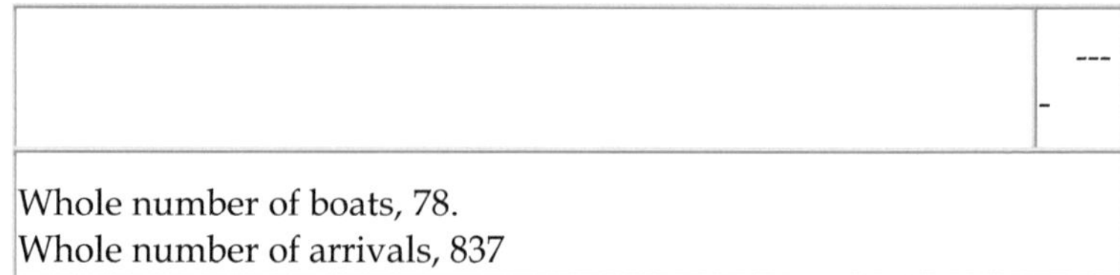

Whole number of boats, 78.
Whole number of arrivals, 837

"It will be seen from the above, that ten more steamers have been engaged in this trade during the present year than last; while in the whole number of arrivals the increase has been two *hundred and sixty-seven.*

"The business on the Minnesota has greatly increased this year. This was to have been expected, considering the great increase in the population of that flourishing portion of our Territory.

"A thriving trade has sprung up between the southern counties of Minnesota, and Galena and Dubuque. During the greater portion of the summer, the War Eagle and Tishimingo run regularly to Winona.

"On the Upper Mississippi there are now three steamers, the Gov. Ramsay, H. M. Rice, and North Star (new). Daring the season these boats ran between St. Anthony and Sauk Rapids."]

It may be well to pause here a moment and inquire into the causes which contribute so wonderfully to build up empire in our north-western domain. The territorial system of the United States has some analogy, it is true, to the colonial system of Great Britain— not the colonial system which existed in the days of the stamp act— but that which a wiser statesmanship has more recently inaugurated. The relation between the general government and our territories is like that of guardian and ward— the relation of a protector, not that of a master. Nor can we find in the history of antiquity any such relationship between colonies and the mother country, whether we consider the system of Phoenicia, where first was exhibited the doctrine of non-intervention, or the tribute-paying colonies of Carthage. That system which was peculiar to Greece, "resting not on state contrivances and economical theories, but on religious sympathies and ancestral associations," came as near perhaps in spirit to ours as any on record. The patronage which the government bestows on new territories is one of the sources of their growth which ought not to be overlooked. Instead of making the territory a dependency and drawing from it a tax, the government pays its political expenses, builds its roads, and gives it a fair start in the world.

Another cause of the successful growth of our territories in general, and of Minnesota in particular, is the ready market which is found in the limits of the territory for everything which can be raised from a generous soil or wrought by industrious hands. The farmer has a ready market for everything that is good to eat or to wear; the artisan is driven by unceasing demands upon his skill. This arises from extensive emigration. Another reason, also, for the rapid growth of the territory, is, that the farmer is not delayed by forests, but finds, outside of pleasant groves of woodland, a smooth, unencumbered soil, ready for the plough the first day he arrives.

But if a salubrious climate, a fertile soil, clear and copious streams, and other material elements, can be reckoned among its physical resources, there are other elements of empire connected with its moral and political welfare which are indispensable. Why is it that Italy is not great? Why is it the South American republics are rusting into abject decay? Is it because they have not enough physical resources, or because their climate is not healthy? Certainly not. It is because their political institutions are rotten and oppressive; because ignorance prevents the growth of a wholesome public opinion. It is the want of the right sort of men and institutions that there is

"Sloth in the mart and schism within the temple."

"Let states that aim at greatness," says Lord Bacon, "take heed how their nobility and gentlemen do multiply too fast; for that maketh the common subject to be a peasant and base swain, driven out of heart, and, in effect, but a gentleman's laborer." He who seeks for the true cause of the greatness and thrift of our northwestern states will find it not less in the influence of just laws and the education of all classes of men, than in the existence of productive fields and in the means of physical wealth.

> "What constitutes a state?
> Not high raised battlement, or labored mound,
>   Thick wall, or moated gate;
> Not cities proud, with spires and turrets crowned;

> Not bays and broad armed ports,
> Where, laughing at the storm, proud navies ride;
> But men, high minded men.

PART II.

TERRITORY OF DACOTAH.

"POPULOUS CITIES AND STATES ARE SPRINGING UP, AS IF BY ENCHANTMENT, FROM THE BOSOM OF OUR WESTERN WILDS."— *The President's Annual Message for* 1856.

THE PROPOSED NEW TERRITORY OF DACOTAH.

Organization of Minnesota as a state— Suggestions as to its division— Views of Captain Pope— Character and resources of the new territory to be left adjoining— Its occupation by the Dacotah Indians— Its organization and name.

THE territory of Minnesota according to its present boundaries embraces an area of 141,839 square miles exclusive of water;— a domain four times as large as the State of Ohio, and twelve times as large as Holland, when her commerce was unrivalled and her fleets ruled the sea. Its limits take in three of the largest rivers of North America; the Mississippi, the Missouri, and the Red River of the North. Though remote from the sea board, ships can go out from its harbors to the ocean in two if not three different channels. Its delightful scenery of lakes and water-falls, of prairie and woodland, are not more alluring to the tourist, than are its invigorating climate and its verdant fields attractive to the husbandman. It has been organized seven years; and its resources have become so much developed, and its population so large, there is a general disposition among the people to have a state organization, and be admitted into the Confederacy of the Union.[1] A measure of this kind is not now premature: on the contrary, it is not for the interest of the general government any longer to defray the expenses of the territory; and the adoption of a state organization, throwing the taxes upon the people, would give rise to a spirit of rivalry and emulation, a watchfulness as to the system of public expenditures, and a more jealous

116

regard for the proper development of the physical resources of the state. The legislature which meets in January (1857), will without doubt take the subject into consideration, and provide for a convention to frame a constitution.

[1 On the 9th of December Mr. Rice, the delegate in congress from Minnesota, gave notice to the house that he would in a few days introduce a bill authorizing the people of the territory to hold a convention for the purpose of forming a state constitution.]

This being the condition of things, the manner in which the territory shall be divided— for no one can expect the new state will embrace the whole extent of the present territory— becomes a very interesting question. Some maintain, I believe, that the territory should be divided by a line running east and west. That would include in its limits the country bordering, for some distance, on the Missouri River; possibly the head of navigation of the Red River of the North. But it is hardly probable that a line of this description would give Minnesota any part of Lake Superior. Others maintain that the territory should be divided by a line running north and south; say, for instance, along the valley of the Red River of the North. Such a division would not give Minnesota any of the Missouri River. But it would have the benefit of the eastern valley of the Red River of the North; of the entire region surrounding the sources of the Mississippi; and of the broad expanse which lies on Lake Superior. The question is highly important, not only to Minnesota, but to the territory which will be left outside of it; and it should be decided with a due regard to the interests of both.[1]

[1 I take pleasure in inserting here a note which I have had the honor to receive from Captain Pope, of the Corps of Topographical Engineers I have before had occasion to quote from the able and instructive report of his exploration of Minnesota.

WASHINGTON, D. C. Dec. 10, 1856.

DEAR SIR:— Your note of the 6th instant is before me; and I will premise my reply by saying that the suggestions I shall offer to your inquiries are based upon my knowledge of the condition of the territory in 1849, which circumstances beyond my acquaintance may have materially modified since.

The important points to be secured for the new state to be erected in the territory of Minnesota, seem to be:— first a harbor on Lake Superior, easily accessible from the West; second, the whole course of the Mississippi to the Iowa line; and, third, the head of navigation of the Red River of the North. It is unnecessary to point out the advantages of securing these features to the new state; and to do so without enclosing too many square miles of territory, I would suggest the following boundaries, viz.:

Commencing on the 49th parallel of latitude, where it is intersected by the Red River of the North, to follow the line of deepest water of that river to the mouth of the Bois des Sioux (or Sioux Wood) River; thence up the middle of that stream to the south-west point of Lake Traverse; thence following a due south line to the northern boundary of the state of Iowa (43 degrees 30' north latitude); thence along this boundary line to the Mississippi River; thence up the middle of the Mississippi River to the mouth of the St. Croix River; thence along the western boundary line of the state of Wisconsin to its intersection with the St. Louis River; thence down the middle of that river to Lake Superior; thence following the coast of the lake to its intersection with the boundary line between the United States and the British possessions, and following this boundary to the place of beginning.

These boundaries will enclose an area of about 65,000 square miles of the best agricultural and manufacturing region in the territory, and will form a state of unrivalled advantages. That portion of the territory set aside by the boundary line will be of little value for many years to come. It presents features differing but little from the region of prairie and table land west of the frontier of Missouri and Arkansas. From this, of course, are to be excepted the western half of the valley of the Red River and of the Big Sioux River, which are as productive as any portion of the territory, which, with the region enclosed between them, would contain arable land sufficient for another state of smaller dimensions.

As you will find stated and fully explained in my report of February, 1850, the valley of the Red River of the North must find an outlet for its productions towards the south, either through the great lakes or by the Mississippi River. The necessity, therefore, of connecting the head of its navigation with a harbor on Lake Superior, and a port on the Mississippi, is sufficiently apparent. As each of these lines of railroad will run through the most fertile and desirable portion of the territory, they will have a value far beyond the mere object of transporting the products of the Red River valley.

The construction of these roads— in fact the mere location of them— will secure a population along the routes at once, and will open a country equal to any in the world.

As these views have been fully elaborated in my report of 1850, I refer you to that paper for the detailed information upon which these views and suggestions are based.

I am sir, respectfully, your obedient servant;

JNO. POPE.
C. C. ANDREWS, Esq.,
Washington, D. C.]

If the division last mentioned— or one on that plan— is made, there will then be left west of the state of Minnesota an extent of country embracing more than half of the territory as it now is; extending from latitude 42 degrees 30' to the 49th degree; and embracing six degrees of longitude— 97th to 103d— at its northern extreme. The Missouri River would constitute nearly the whole of its western boundary. In the northerly part the Mouse and Pembina Rivers are among its largest streams; in the middle flows the large and finely wooded Shayenne, "whose valley possesses a fertile soil and offers many inducements to its settlement;" while towards the south it would have the Jacques, the Big Sioux, the Vermillion, and the head waters of the St. Peter's. In its supply of copious streams, nature seems there to have been lavish. Of the Big Sioux River, M. Nicollet says, its Indian name means that it is continuously lined with wood; that its length cannot be less than three hundred and fifty miles. "It flows through a beautiful and fertile country; amidst which the Dacotahs, inhabiting the valleys of the St. Peter's and Missouri, have always kept up summer establishments on the borders of the adjoining lakes, whilst they hunted the river banks. Buffalo herds are confidently expected to be met with here at all seasons of the year." The Jacques (the Indian name of which is *Tchansansan*) "takes its rise on the plateau of the Missouri beyond the parallel of 47 degrees north; and after pursuing nearly a north and south course, empties into the Missouri River below 43 degrees. It is deemed navigable with small hunting canoes for between five hundred and six hundred miles; but below *Otuhuoja*, it will float much larger boats. The shores of the river are generally tolerably well wooded, though only at intervals. Along those portions where it widens into lakes, very eligible situations for farms would be found." The same explorer says, the most important tributary of the Jacques is the Elm River, which "might not deserve any special mention as a navigable stream, but is very well worthy of notice on account of the timber growing on its own banks and those of its forks." He further observes (Report, p. 46) that "the basin of the river Jacques, between the two coteaux and in the latitude of *Otuhuoja*, may be laid down as having a breadth of eighty miles, sloping gradually down from an elevation of seven hundred to seven hundred and fifty feet. These dimensions, of course, vary in the different parts of the valley; but what I have said will convey some idea of the immense prairie watered by the *Tchan-sansan*, which has been deemed by all travellers to those distant regions perhaps the most beautiful within the territory of the United States."

The middle and northern part comprises an elevated plain, of average fertility and tolerably wooded. Towards the south it is characterized by bold undulations. The valley of the Missouri is narrow; and the bluffs which border upon it are abrupt and high. The country is adapted to agricultural pursuits, and though inferior as a general thing to much of Minnesota, affords promise of thrift and property in its future. It is blessed with a salubrious climate. Dr. Suckley, who accompanied the expedition of Gov. Stevens through that part of the West, as far as Puget Sound, says in his official report: "On reviewing the whole route, the unequalled and unparalleled good health of the command during a march of over eighteen hundred miles appears remarkable; especially when we consider the hardships and exposures necessarily incident to such a trip. Not a case of ague or fever occurred. Such a state of health could only be accounted for by the great salubrity of the countries passed through, and their freedom from malarious or other endemic disease."

Governor Stevens has some comprehensive remarks concerning that part of the country in his report. "The Grand Plateau of the Bois des Sioux and the Mouse River valley are the two keys of railroad communication from the Mississippi River westward through the territory of Minnesota. The Bois des Sioux is a river believed to be navigable for steamers of light draught, flowing northward from Lake Traverse into the Red River of the North, and the plateau of the Bois des Sioux may be considered as extending from south of Lake Traverse to the south bend of the Red River, and from the Rabbit River, some thirty miles east of the Bois des Sioux River, to the Dead Colt hillock. This plateau separates the rivers flowing into Hudson's Bay from those flowing into the Mississippi River. The Mouse River valley, in the western portion of Minnesota, is from ten to twenty miles broad; is separated from the Missouri River by the Coteau du Missouri, some six hundred feet high, and it is about the same level as the parallel valley of the Missouri." (Report, ch. 4.)

M. Nicollet was a scientific or matter of fact man, who preferred to talk about "erratic blocks" and "cretaceous formations" rather than to indulge in poetic descriptions. The outline which follows, however, of the western part of the territory is what he considers "a faint description of this beautiful country." "The basin of the Upper Mississippi is separated in a great part of its extent from that of the Missouri, by an elevated plain; the appearance of which, seen from the valley of the St. Peter's or that of the Jacques, looming as it were a distant shore, has suggested for it the name of *Coteau des Prairies*. Its more appropriate designation would be that of *plateau*, which means something more than is conveyed to the mind by the expression, a *plain*. Its northern extremity is in latitude 46 degrees, extending to 43 degrees; after which it loses its distinctive elevation above the surrounding plains, and passes into rolling prairies. Its length is about two hundred miles, and its general direction N. N. W. and S. S. E. Its northern termination (called *Tete du Couteau* in consequence of its peculiar configuration) is not more than fifteen to twenty miles across; its elevation above the level of the Big Stone Lake is eight hundred and ninety feet, and above the ocean one thousand nine hundred and sixteen feet. Starting from this extremity (that is, the head of the Coteau), the surface of the plateau is undulating, forming many dividing ridges which separate the waters flowing into the St. Peter's and the Mississippi from those of the Missouri. Under the 44th degree of latitude, the breadth of the Coteau is about forty miles, and its mean elevation is here reduced to one thousand four hundred and fifty feet above the sea. Within this space its two slopes are rather abrupt, crowned with verdure, and scolloped by deep ravines thickly shaded with bushes, forming the beds of rivulets that water the subjacent plains.

The Coteau itself is isolated, in the midst of boundless and fertile prairies, extending to the west, to the north, and into the valley of the St. Peter's.

The plain at its northern extremity is a most beautiful tract of land diversified by hills, dales, woodland, and lakes, the latter abounding in fish. This region of country is probably the most elevated between the Gulf of Mexico and Hudson's Bay. From its summit, proceeding from its western to its eastern limits, grand views are afforded. At its eastern border particularly, the prospect is magnificent beyond description, extending over the immense green turf that forms the basin of the Red River of the North, the forest-capped summits of the *haugeurs des terres* that surround the sources of the Mississippi, the granitic valley of the Upper St. Peter's, and the depressions in which are Lake Traverse and the Big Stone Lake. There can be no doubt that in future times this region will be the summer resort of the wealthy of the land." (pp. 9, 10.)

I will pass over what he says of the "vast and magnificent valley of the Red River of the North," having before given some account of that region, and merely give his description of the largest lake which lies in the northern part of the territory: "The greatest extension of Devil's Lake is at least forty miles,— but may be more, as we did not, and could not, ascertain the end of the north-west bay, which I left undefined on the map. It is bordered by hills that are pretty well wooded on one side, but furrowed by ravines and coulees, that are taken advantage of by warlike parties, both for attack and defence according to circumstances. The lake itself is so filled up with islands and promontories, that, in travelling along its shores, it is only occasionally that one gets a glimpse of its expanse. This description belongs only to its wooded side; for, on the opposite side, the shores, though still bounded by hills, are destitute of trees, so as to exhibit an embankment to the east from ten to twelve miles long, upon an average breadth of three-quarters of a mile. The average breadth of the lake may be laid down at fifteen miles. Its waters appear to be the drainings of the surrounding hills. We discovered no outlets in the whole extent of about three-quarters of its contour we could explore. At all events, if there be any they do not empty into the Red River of the North, since the lake is shut up in that direction, and since we found its true geographical position to be much more to the north than it is ordinarily laid down upon maps. A single depression at its lower end would intimate that, in times of high water, some discharge might possibly take place; but then it would be into the *Shayenne*." (p. 50.)

Such are some of the geographical outlines of the extensive domain which will be soon organized as a new territory.

What will it be called? If the practice hitherto followed of applying to territories the names which they have been called by their aboriginal inhabitants is still adhered to, this new territory will have the name of Dacotah. It is the correct or Indian name of those tribes whom we call the Sioux; the latter being an unmeaning Indian-French word. Dacotah means "united people," and is the word which the Indians apply to seven of their bands.[1] These tribes formerly occupied the country south and south-west of Lake Superior; from whence they were gradually driven towards the Missouri and the Rocky Mountains by their powerful and dreaded enemies the Chippewas. Since which time they have been the acknowledged occupants of the broad region to which they have impressed a name. Several of the tribes, however, have crossed the Missouri, between which and the Rocky Mountains they still linger a barbaric life. We may now hope to realize the truth of Hiawatha's words:—

> "After many years of warfare,
> Many years of strife and bloodshed,
> There is peace between the Ojibways
> And the tribe of the Dacotahs."

[1 The following description of the Dacotahs is based on observations made in 1823. "The Dacotahs are a large and powerful nation of Indians, distinct in their manners, language, habits, and opinions, from the Chippewas, Sauks, Foxes, and Naheawak or Kilisteno, as well as from all nations of the Algonquin stock. They are likewise unlike the Pawnees and the Minnetarees or Gros Ventres. They inhabit a large district of country which may be comprised within the following limits: — From Prairie du Chien, on the Mississippi, by a curved line extending east of north and made to include all the eastern tributaries of the Mississippi, to the first branch of Chippewa River; the head waters of that stream being claimed by the Chippewa Indians; thence by a line running west of north to the head of Spirit Lake; thence by a westerly line to the Riveree de Corbeau; thence up that river to its head, near Otter Tail Lake; thence by a westerly line to Red River, and down that river to Pembina; thence by a south-westerly line to the east bank of the Missouri near the Mandan villages; thence down the Missouri to a point probably not far from Soldier's River; thence by a line running east of north to Prairie du Chien.

This immense extent of country is inhabited by a nation calling themselves, in their internal relations, the Dacotah, which means the Allied; but who, in their external relations, style themselves the Ochente Shakoan, which signifies the nation of seven (council) fires. This refers to the following division which formerly prevailed among them, viz.: —
 1. Mende-Wahkan-toan, or people of the Spirit Lake.
 2. Wahkpa-toan, or people of the leaves.
 3. Sisi-toan, or Miakechakesa.
 4. Yank-toan-an, or Fern leaves
 5. Yank-toan, or descended from the Fern leaves.
 6. Ti-toan, or Braggers.
 7. Wahkpako-toan, or the people that shoot at leaves.

 — Long's *Expedition to Sources of St. Peter's River &c.*, vol. 1, pp. 376, 378.]

If it be asked what will be done with these tribes when the country comes to be settled, I would observe, as I have said, that the present policy of the government is to procure their settlement on reservations. This limits them to smaller boundaries; and tends favorably to their civilization. I might also say here, that the title which the Indians have to the country they occupy is that of occupancy. They have the natural right to occupy the land; but the absolute and sovereign title is in the United States. The Indians can dispose of their title to no party or power but the United States. When, however, the government wishes to extinguish their title of occupancy, it pays them a fair price for their lands according as may be provided by treaty. The policy of our government towards the Indians is eminently that of protection and preservation; not of conquest and extermination.

Dacotah is the name now applied to the western part of Minnesota, and I am assured by the best informed men of that section, that such will be the name of the territory when organized.

PART III.

TABLE OF STATISTICS.

I. LIST OF POST OFFICES AND POSTMASTERS IN MINNESOTA.
II. LAND OFFICES, &c.
III. NEWSPAPERS PUBLISHED IN MINNESOTA.
IV. TABLE OF DISTANCES.

I.

POST OFFICES AND POSTMASTERS.

I HAVE been furnished, at brief notice, with the following accurate list of the Post Offices and Postmasters in Minnesota by my very excellent friend, Mr. JOHN N. OLIVIER, of the Sixth Auditor's Office:

LIST OF POST OFFICES AND POSTMASTERS IN THE TERRITORY OF MINNESOTA, PREPARED PROM THE BOOKS OF THE APPOINTMENT OFFICE, POST OFFICE DEPARTMENT, TO DECEMBER 12, 1856.

Post Office.	Postmaster.
BENTON COUNTY.	
Belle Prairie	Calvin C. Hicks.
Big Lake	Joseph Brown.

Clear Lake	F. E. Baldwin.
Crow Wing	Allen Morrison.
Elk River	John Q. A. Nickerson.
Itasca	John C. Bowers.
Little Falls	C. H. Churchill.
Royalton	Rodolph's D. Kinney.
Sauk Rapids	C. B. Vanstest.
Swan River	James Warren.
Watab	David Gilman.

BLUE EARTH COUNTY.

Kasota	Isaac Allen.
Mankato	Parsons K. Johnson.
Liberty	Edward Brace.
Pajutazee	Andrew Robertson.
South Bend	Matthew Thompson.
Winnebago Agency	Henry Foster.

BROWN COUNTY.

| New Ulm | Anton Kans. |

Sioux Agency	Asa W. Daniels.

CARVER COUNTY.

Carver	Joseph A. Sargent.
Chaska	Timothy D. Smith.
La Belle	Isaac Berfield.
Scandia	A. Bergquest.
San Francisco	James B. Cotton.
Young America	R. M. Kennedy.

CHISAGO COUNTY.

Amador	Lorenzo A. Lowden.
Cedar Creek	Samuel Wyatt.
Chippewa	J. P. Gulding.
Chisago City	Henry S. Cluiger.
Hanley	John Hanley.
Rushseby	George B. Folsom.
Sunrise City	George S. Frost.
Taylor's Falls	Peter E. Walker.
Wyoming	Jordan Egle.

DAKOTA COUNTY.

Athens	Jacob Whittemore.
Centralia	H. P. Sweet.
Empire City	Ralph P. Hamilton.
Farmington	Noredon Amedon.
Fort Snelling	Franklin Steele.
Hampton	James Archer.
Hastings	John F. Marsh.
Lakeville	Samuel P. Baker.
Le Sueur	Kostum K. Peck.
Lewiston	Stephen N. Carey.
Mendota	Hypolite Dupues.
Ninninger	Louis Loichot.
Ottowa	Frank Y. Hoffstott.
Rosemount	Andrew Keegan.
Vermillion	Leonard Aldrich.
Waterford	Warren Atkinson.

DODGE COUNTY.

Avon	Noah F. Berry.
Ashland	George Townsend.
Claremont	Goerge Hitchcock.
Concord	James M. Sumner.
Montorville	John H. Shober.
Wasioga	Eli. P. Waterman.
FAIRBAULT COUNTY.	
Blue Earth City	George B. Kingsley.
Verona	Newell Dewey.
FILLMORE COUNTY.	
Bellville	Wilson Bell.
Big Spring	William Walter.
Chatfield	Edwin B. Gere.
Clarimona	Wm. F. Strong.
Deer Creek	William S. Hill.
Elkhorn	Jacob McQuillan.
Elliota	John C. Cleghorn.
Etna	O. B. Bryant.

Fairview	John G. Bouldin.
Fillmore	Robert Rea.
Forestville	Forest Henry.
Jordan	James M. Gilliss.
Lenora	Chas. B. Wilford.
Looking Glass	Lemuel Jones.
Newburg	Gabriel Gabrielson.
Odessa	Jacob P. Kennedy.
Peterson	Knud Peterson.
Pilot Mound	Daniel B. Smith.
Preston	L. Preston.
Riceford	Wm. D. Vandoren.
Richland	Benjn. F. Tillotson.
Rushford	Sylvester S. Stebbins.
Spring Valley	Condello Wilkins.
Uxbridge	Daniel Crowell.
Waukokee	John M. West.

FREEBORN COUNTY.

Albert Lea	Lorenzo Murray.
Geneva	John Heath.
St. Nicholas	Saml. M. Thompson.
Shell Rock	Edward P. Skinner.

GOODHUE COUNTY.

Burr Oak Springs	Henry Doyle.
Cannon River Falls	George McKenzie.
Central Point	Charles W. Hackett.
Pine Island	John Chance.
Poplar Grove	John Lee.
Red Wing	Henry C. Hoffman.
Spencer	Hans Mattson.
Wacouta	George Post.
Westervelt	Evert Westervelt.

HENNEPIN COUNTY.

Bloomington	Reuben B. Gibson.
Chanhassen	Henry M. Lyman.
Dayton	John Baxter.

Eden Prairie	Jonas Staring.
Elm Creek	Charles Miles.
Harmony	James A. Dunsmore.
Excelsior	Charles P. Smith.
Island City	William F. Russell.
Maple Plain	Irvin Shrewsbury.
Medicine Lake	Francis Hagot.
Minneapolis	Alfred E. Ames.
Minnetonka	Levi W. Eastman.
Osseo	Warren Samson.
Perkinsville	N. T. Perkins.
Watertown	Alexander Moore.
Wyzata	W. H. Chapman.
HOUSTON COUNTY.	
Brownsville	Charles Brown.
Caledonia	Wm. J. McKee.
Hamilton	Charles Smith.
Hackett's Grove	Emery Hackett.

Hokah	Edward Thompson.
Houston	Ole Knudson.
Loretta	Edmund S. Lore.
Looneyville	Daniel Wilson.
La Crescent	William Gillett.
Mooney Creek	Cyrus B. Sinclair.
Portland	Alexr. Batcheller.
Sheldon	John Paddock.
Spring Grove	Embric Knudson.
San Jacinto	George Canon.
Wiscoy	Benton Aldrich.
Yucatan	T. A. Pope.
LAKE COUNTY.	
Burlington	Chas. B. Harbord.
LA SUEUR COUNTY.	
Elysium	Silas S. Munday.
Grandville	Bartlet Y. Couch.
Lexington	Henry Earl.

Waterville	Samuel D. Drake.

McLEOD COUNTY.

Glencoe	Surman G. Simmons.
Hutchinson	Lewis Harrington.

MEEKER COUNTY.

Forest City	Walter C. Bacon.

MORRISON COUNTY.

Little Falls	Orlando A. Churchill.

MOWER COUNTY.

Austin	Alanson B. Vaughan.
Frankford	Lewis Patchin.
High Forest	Thos. H. Armstrong.
Le Roy	Daniel Caswell.

NICOLLET COUNTY.

Eureka	Edwin Clark.
Hilo	William Dupray.
Saint Peter	George Hezlep.
Travers des Sioux	William Huey.

OLMSTEAD COUNTY.

Durango	Samuel Brink.
Kalmar	James A. Blair.
Oronoco	Samuel P. Hicks.
Pleasant Grove	Samuel Barrows.
Rochester	Phineas H. Durfel.
Salem	Cyrus Holt.
Springfield	Almon H. Smith.
Waterloo	Robert S. Latta.
Zumbro	Lucy Cobb.

PEMBINA COUNTY.

Cap Lake	David B. Spencer.
Pembina	Joseph Rolette.
Red Lake	Sela G. Wright.
Saint Joseph's	George A. Belcourt.

PIERCE COUNTY.

Fort Ridgeley	Benjn. H. Randall.

PINE COUNTY.

Alhambra	Herman Trott.
Mille Lac	Mark Leadbetter.

RAMSEY COUNTY.

Anoka	Arthur Davis.
Centreville	Charles Pettin.
Columbus	John Klerman.
Howard's Lake	John P. Howard.
Little Canada	Walter B. Boyd.
Manomine	Joseph A. Willis.
Otter Lake	Ross Wilkinson.
Red Rock	Giles H. Fowler.
St. Anthony's Falls	Norton H. Hemiup.
St. Paul	Charles S. Cave.

RICE COUNTY.

Cannon City	C. Smith House.
Faribault	Alexander Faribault.
Medford	Smith Johnson.
Morristown	Walter Norris.

Northfield	Calvin S. Short.
Shieldsville	Joshua Tufts.
Union Lake	Henry M. Humphrey.
Walcott	Joseph Richardson.

SAINT LOUIS COUNTY.

Falls of St. Louis	Joseph Y. Buckner.
Oneota	Edmund F. Ely.
Twin Lakes	George W. Perry.

SCOTT COUNTY.

Belle Plaine	Nahum Stone.
Louisville	Joseph R. Ashley.
Mount Pleasant	John Soules.
New Dublin	Dominick McDermott
Sand Creek	William Holmes.
Shak-a-pay	Reuben M. Wright.

SIBLEY COUNTY.

Henderson	Henry Pochler.
Prairie Mound	Morgan Lacey.

STEARNS COUNTY.

Clinton	John H. Linneman.
Neenah	Henry B. Johnson.
Saint Cloud	Joseph Edelbrook.
Torah	Reuben M. Richardson.

STEELE COUNTY.

Adamsville	Hiram Pitcher.
Aurora	Charles Adsit.
Dodge City	John Coburn.
Ellwood	Wilber F. Fiske.
Josco	James Hanes.
Lemond	Abram Fitzsimmons.
Owatana	Samuel B. Smith.
St. Mary's	Horatio B. Morrison.
Swavesey	Andrew J. Bell.
Wilton	David J. Jenkins.

SUPERIOR COUNTY.

Beaver Bay	Robert McLean.

French River	F. W. Watrous.
Grand Marias	Richard Godfrey.
Grand Portage	H. H. McCullough.
WABASHAW COUNTY.	
Greenville	Rodman Benchard.
Independence	Seth L. McCarty.
Lake City	Harvey F. Williamson.
Mazeppa	John E. Hyde.
Minneska	Nathaniel F. Tifft.
Minnesota City	Samuel E. Cotton.
Mount Vernon	Stephen M. Burns.
Reed's Landing	Fordyce S. Richard.
Wabashaw	J. F. Byrne.
West Newton	Austin R. Swan.
WAHNATAH COUNTY.	
Fort Ripley	Solon W. Manney.
WASHINGTON COUNTY.	
Cottage Grove	Stephen F. Douglass.

Lake Land	Freeman C. Tyler.
Marine Mills	Orange Walker.
Milton Mills	Lemuel Bolles.
Point Douglass	R. R. Henry.
Stillwater	Harley Curtis.

WINONA COUNTY.

Dacota	Nathan Brown.
Eagle Bluffs	William W. Bennett.
Homer	John A. Torrey.
New Boston	William H. Dwight.
Richmond	Samuel C. Dick.
Ridgeway	Joseph Cooper.
Saint Charles	Lewis H. Springer.
Saratoga	Thomas P. Dixon.
Stockton	William C. Dodge.
Twin Grove	Oren Cavath.
Utica	John W. Bentley.
Warren	Eben B. Jewett.

Winona	John W. Downer.
White Water Falls	Miles Pease.
WRIGHT COUNTY.	
Berlin	Charles W. Lambert
Buffalo	Amasa Ackley.
Clear Water	Simon Stevens.
Monticello	M. Fox.
Northwood	A. H. Kelly.
Rockford	Joel Florida.
Silver Creek	Abram G. Descent.

II.

LIST OF LAND OFFICES AND OFFICERS IN MINNESOTA.

GENERAL LAND OFFICE,

December 8, 1856.

SIR: Your two letters of the 6th instant, asking for a list of the land offices in Minnesota Territory, with the names of the officers connected therewith,— also the number of acres sold and the amount of fees received by such officers, during the fiscal year, ending 30th June, 1856, have been received.

In reply, I herewith enclose a statement of the information desired, save that the amount of fees for the fiscal year cannot be stated.

Very respectfully,

THOMAS A. HENDRICKS,

Commissioner,

C. C. ANDREWS, Esq.

LIST OF LAND OFFICES AND OFFICERS IN MINNESOTA.				
LAND DI-STRICTS.	Name of Register	Name of Receiver.	Number of acres sold during the fiscal year ending 30th of June, 1856.	Amount of purchase-money received therefor.
Stillwater	Thos. M. Fullerton	Wm. Holcomb	103,141.31	128,930.23
Sauk Rapids	Geo. W. Sweet	Wm. H. Wood	49,712.44	65,355.41
Chatfield (late Brownsville)	John R. Bennet	Jno. H. McKenny	238,323.26	298,920.90
Minneapolis	Marcus P. Olds	Roswell P. Russell	139,188.96	186,651.77
Winona	Diedrich Upman	Lorenzo D. Smith	264,777.38	335,845.66
Red Wing	Wm. P. Phelps	Chr. Graham	206,987.32	265,173.84
			1,002,130.67	$1,280,867.81

Since the 30th June, 1856, the following offices have been established and officers appointed.

| Buchanan | Saml. Clark | John Whipple |
| Ojibeway | Saml. Plumer | Wm. Sawyer |

III.

LIST OF NEWSPAPERS PUBLISHED IN MINNESOTA.		
PIONEER AND DEMOCRAT	St. Paul	Daily and Weekly
MINNESOTIAN	St. Paul	Daily and Weekly
TIMES	St. Paul	Daily and Weekly
FINANCIAL ADVERTISER	St. Paul	Weekly
UNION	Stillwater	Weekly
MESSENGER	Stillwater	Weekly
EXPRESS	St. Anthony	Weekly
REPUBLICAN	St. Anthony	Weekly
DEMOCRAT	Minneapolis	Weekly
FRONTIERSMAN	Sauk Rapids	Weekly
NORTHERN HERALD	Watab	Weekly

INDEPENDENT	Shakopee	Weekly
REPUBLICAN	Shakopee	Weekly
DEMOCRAT	Henderson	Weekly
COURIER	St. Peter	Weekly
DAKOTA JOURNAL	Hastings	Weekly
SENTINEL	Red Wing	Weekly
GAZETTE	Canon Falls	Weekly
JOURNAL	Wabashaw	Weekly
ARGUS	Winona	Weekly
REPUBLICAN	Winona	Weekly
SOUTHERN HERALD	Brownsville	Weekly
	Carimona	Weekly
DEMOCRAT	Chatfield	Weekly
REPUBLICAN	Chatfield	Weekly
RICE COUNTY HERALD	Faribault	Weekly
	St. Cloud	Weekly

OWATONIA WATCHMAN AND REGISTER	Owatonia	Weekly.

IV.

TABLE OF DISTANCES.

TABLE OF DISTANCES FROM ST. PAUL.		
	MILES	
To St. Anthony	8 3/4	
Rice Creek	7	15 3/4
St. Francis, or Rum River	9	25
Itasca	7	32
Elk River	6	38
Big Lake	10	48
Big Meadow (Sturgis)	18	66
St. Cloud (Sauk Rapids)	10	76
Watab	6	82
Little Rock	2	84
Platte River	12	96
Swan River	10	106

Little Falls	3	109
Belle Prairie	5	114
Fort Ripley	10	124
Crow Wing River	6	130
Sandy Lake	120	250
Savannah Portage	15	265
Across the Portage	5	270
Down Savannah River to St. Louis River	20	290
Fond-du-Lac	60	350
Lake Superior	22	372
Crow Wing River	130	
Otter Tail Lake	70	200
Rice River	74	274
Sand Hills River	70	340
Grand Fork, Red River	40	380
Pembina	80	460
Sandy Lake	250	
Leech Lake	150	400

Red Lake	80	480
Pembrina	150	630
Stillwater	18	
Arcola	5	23
Marine Mills	6	29
Falls St. Croix	19	48
Pokagema	40	88
Fond-du-Lac	75	164
Red Rock	6	
Point Douglass	24	
Red Wing		
Winona's Rock, Lake Pepin	30	60
Wabashaw	30	90
Prairie du Chien	145	235
Cassville	29	264
Peru	21	285
Dubuque	8	293
Mouth of Fever River	17	310

Rock Island	52	362
Burlington	135	497
Keokuk	53	550
St. Louis	179	729
Cairo	172	901
New Orleans	1040	1941
Mendota	7	
Black Dog Village	4	
Sixe's Village	21	
Traverse des Sioux	50	
Little Rock	45	
Lac Qui Parle	80	
Big Stone Lake	66	
Fort Pierce, on Missouri	240	

TABLE OF DISTANCES FROM ST. CLOUD.

To Minneapolis	62
Superior City, on Brott and Wilson's Road	120
Traverse des Sioux	70

Henderson	60
Fort Ridgley	100
Long Prairie	40
Otter Tail Lake	60
The Salt Springs	120
Fort Ripley	60
Mille Lac City	60
DISTANCES FROM CROW WING.	
To Chippeway Mission	15
Ojibeway	50
Superior City	80
Otter Tail City	60
St. Cloud	55

PART IV.

PREEMPTION FOR CITY OR TOWN SITES.

PREEMPTION FOR CITY OR TOWN SITES.

AT a late moment, and while the volume is in press, I am enabled to present the following exposition of the Preemption Law, addressed to the Secretary of the Interior by Mr. Attorney-General

Cushing. (See "Opinions of Attorneys General," vol. 7, 733-743 — in press.)

PREEMPTION FOR CITY OR TOWN SITES.

Portions of the public lands, to the amount of three hundred and twenty acres, may be taken up by individuals or preemptioners for city or town sites.

The same rules as to proof of occupation apply in the case of municipal, as of agricultural, preemption.

The statute assumes that the purposes of a city or town have preference over those of trade or of agriculture.

ATTORNEY GENERAL'S OFFICE

July 2, 1856.

SIR: Your communication of the 20th May, transmitting papers regarding Superior City (so called) in the State of Wisconsin, submits for consideration three precise questions of law; two of them presenting inquiry of the legal relations of locations for town sites on the public domain, and the third presenting inquiry of another matter, which, although pertinent to the case, yet is comprehended in a perfectly distinct class of legal relations.

I propose, in this communication, to reply only upon the two first questions.

The act of Congress of April 24, 1841, entitled "An act to appropriate the proceeds of the sales of the public lands and to grant preemption rights," contains, in section 10th, the following provisions: "no lands reserved for the support of schools, nor lands acquired by either of the two last treaties with the Miami tribe of Indians in the State of Indiana, or which may be acquired of the Wyandot tribe of Indians in the State of Ohio, or other Indian reservation to which the title has been or may be extinguished by the United States at any time during the operation of this act; no sections of lands reserved to the United States alternate to other sections of land granted to any of the States for the construction of any canal, railroad, or other public improvement; no sections or fractions of sections included within the limits of any incorporated town; no portions of the public lands which have been selected for the site of a city or town; no parcel of a lot of land actually settled or occupied for the purposes of trade and not agriculture; and no lands on which are situated any known salines or mines, shall be liable to entry under or by virtue of this act." (v Stat. at Large, p. 456.)

An act passed May 28, 1844, entitled "An act for the relief of citizens of towns upon the lands of the United States under certain circumstances," provides as follows:

"That whenever any portion of the surveyed public lands has been or shall be settled upon and occupied as a town site, and therefore not subject to entry under the existing preemption laws, it shall be lawful, in case such town or place shall be incorporated, for the corporate authorities thereof, and if not incorporated, for the judges of the county court for the county in which such town may be situated, to enter at the proper land office, and at the minimum price, the land so settled and occupied, in trust for the several use and benefit of the several occupants thereof, according to their respective interests; the execution of which trust, as to the disposal of the lots in said town, and the proceeds of the sales thereof, to be conducted under such rules and regulations as may be prescribed by the legislative authority of the state or territory in which the same is situated; *Provided,* that the entry of the land intended by this act be made prior to the commencement of a public sale of the body of land in which it is included, and that the entry shall include only such land as is actually occupied by the town, and be made in conformity to the legal subdivisions of the public lands authorized by the act of the twenty-fourth of April, one thousand eight hundred and twenty, and shall not in the whole exceed three hundred and twenty acres; and *Provided* also, that the act of the said trustees, not made in conformity to the rules and regulations herein alluded to, shall be void and of none effect:" * * * (v Stat. at Large, p. 687.)

Upon which statutes you present the following questions of construction: "1st. What is the legal signification to be given to the words, 'portions of the public lands which have been selected as the site for a city or town,' which occur in the preemption law of 1841, and which portions of the public lands are by said act exempted from its provisions? Do they authorize selections by individuals with a view to the building thereon of a city or town, or do they contemplate a selection made by authority of some special law?

"Do the words in the act of 23d May, 1844, 'and that the entry shall include only such land as is actually occupied by the town,' restrict the entry to those quarter quarter-sections, or forty acre subdivisions, alone, on which houses have been erected as part of said town, or do they mean, only, that the entry shall not embrace any land not shown *by* the survey on the ground, or the plat of the town, to be occupied thereby, and not to exceed 820 acres, which is to be taken by legal subdivisions, according to the public survey, and to what species of 'legal subdivisions' is reference made in said act of 1844?"

These questions, as thus presented by you, are abstract questions of law,— namely, of the construction of statutes. They are distinctly and clearly stated, so as not to require of me any investigation of external facts to render them more intelligible. Nor do they require of me to attempt to make application of them to any actual case, conflict of right, or controversy either between private individuals or such individuals and the Government.

It is true that, accompanying your communication, there is a great mass of representations, depositions, arguments, and other papers, which show that the questions propounded by you are not speculative ones, and that, on the contrary, they bear, in some way, on matters of interest, public or private, to be decided by the Department. But those are matters for you, not for me, to determine. You have requested my opinion of certain points of law, to be used by you, so far as you see fit, in aid of such your own determination. I am thus happily relieved of the task of examining and undertaking to analyze the voluminous documents in the case: more especially as your questions, while precise and complete in themselves, derive all needful illustration from the very instructive report in the case of the present Commissioner of Public Lands and the able brief on the subject drawn up in your Department.

I. To return to the questions before me: the first is in substance whether the words in the act of 1841,— " portions of the public land which have been selected as the site for a city or a town,"— are to be confined to cases of such selection in virtue of some special authority, or by some official authority?

I think not, for the following reasons:

The statute does not by any words of legal intendment say so.

The next preceding clause of the act, which speaks of lands "included within the limits of any incorporated town," implies the contrary, in making separate provision for a township existing by special or public authority.

The next succeeding clause, which speaks of land "actually settled or occupied for the purposes of trade and not agriculture," leads to the same conclusion; for why should selection for a town site require special authority any more than occupation for the purposes of trade?

The general scope of the act has the same tendency. Its general object is to regulate, in behalf of individuals, the acquisition of the public domain by preemption, after voluntary occupation for a certain period of time, and under other prescribed circumstances. In doing this, it gives a preference preemption to certain other uses of the public land, by excluding such land from liability to ordinary preemption. Among the uses thus privileged, and to which precedence in preemption is accorded, are, 1. "Sections, or fractions of sections included within the limits of any incorporated town;" 2. "Portions of the public land which have been selected for the site of a city or town;" and, 3. "Land actually settled or occupied for the purposes of trade, and not agriculture." Now, it is not easy to see any good reason why, if individuals may thus take voluntarily for the purposes of agriculture,— they may not also take for the purposes of a city or town. The statute assumes that the purposes of a city or town have preference over those of trade, and still more over those of agriculture. Yet individuals may take for either of the latter objects: *a fortiori* they may take for a city or town.

Why should it be assumed that individual action in this respect is prohibited for towns any more than for trade or agriculture? It does not concern the Government whether two persons preempt one hundred and sixty acres each for the purposes of agriculture, or for the purpose of a town, except that the latter object will, incidentally, be more beneficial to the Government. Nor is there any other consideration of public policy to induce the Government to endeavor to discourage the formation of towns. Why, then, object to individuals taking up a given quantity of land in one case rather than in the other?

Finally, the act of 1844 definitively construes the act of 1841, and proves that the "selection" for town sites there spoken of may be either by public authority or by individuals: — that the word is for that reason designedly general, and without qualification, but must be fixed by occupation. That act supposes public land to be "settled upon and occupied as a town site," and "therefore" not subject to entry under the existing preemption laws. This description identifies it with the land "selected for the site of *a city* or town," in the previous act. It limits the quantity so to be selected, that is, settled or occupied, to three hundred and twenty acres, and otherwise regulates the selection as hereinafter explained. It then provides how such town site is to be entered and patented. If the town be incorporated, then the *entry* is to be made by its corporate authorities. If the town be not incorporated, then it may be entered in the name of the judges of the county court of the county, in which the projected town lies, "in trust for the several use and benefit of the several occupants thereof, according to their respective interests." Here we have express recognition of voluntary selection and occupancy by individuals, and provision for means by which legal title in their behalf may be acquired and patented.

I am aware that by numerous statutes anterior to the act of 1841, provision is made for the *authoritative* selection of town sites in special cases; but such provisions do by no means exclude or contradict the later enactment of a general provision of law to comprehend all cases of selections for town sites, whether authoritative or voluntary. I think the act of 1841, construed in the light of the complementary act of 1844, as it must be, provides clearly for both contingencies or conditions of the subject. Among the anterior acts, however, is one of great importance and significancy upon this point, more especially as that act received exposition at the time from the proper departments of the Government. I allude to the act of June 22d, 1838, entitled "An act to grant preemption rights to settlers on the public lands." This act, like that of 1841, contains a provision reserving certain lands from ordinary preemption, among which are:

"Any portions of public lands, surveyed or otherwise, which have been actually selected as sites for cities or towns, lotted into smaller quantities than eighty acres, and settled upon and occupied for the purposes of trade, and not of agricultural cultivation and improvement, or any land specially occupied or reserved for town lots, or other purposes, by authority of the United States." (v Stat. at Large, p. 251.)

Here the "selection" generally, and the "selection" by authority are each provided for *eo nomine*. It is obvious that the provision in the latter case is made for certainty only; since, by the general rules of statute construction, no ordinary claim of preemption could attach to reservations made by authority of the United States. The effective provision in the enactment quoted, must be selections not made by the authority of the United States.

In point of fact the provision was construed by the Department to include all voluntary selections: lands, says the circular of the General Land Office of July 8, 1838, "which settlers have selected with a view of building thereon a village or city."

It seems to me that the same considerations which induced this construction of the word "selection" in the act of 1838, dictate a similar construction of the same word in the subsequent act. Besides which, when a word or words of a statute, which were of uncertain signification originally, but which have been construed by the proper authority, are repented in a subsequent statute, that is understood as being not a repetition merely of the word with the received construction, but an implied legislative adoption even of such construction.

II. The second question is of the construction of the act of 1844, supplemental to that of 1841; and as the construction of the elder derives aid from the language of the later one, so does that of the latter from the former. The question is divisible into sub-questions.

1. Does the phrase "that the entry (for a town-site) shall include only such land as is actually occupied by the town," restrict the

entry to those quarter quarter-sections, or forty acre subdivisions alone, on which houses have been erected as part of said town?

2. What is the meaning of the phrase in the act "legal subdivisions of the public lands," in "conformity" with which the entry must be made?

I put the two acts together and find that they provide for a system of preemptions for, among other things, agricultural occupation, commercial or mechanical occupation, and municipal occupation.

In regard to agricultural occupation, the laws provide that, in certain cases and conditions, one person may preempt one hundred and sixty acres, and that in regard to municipal occupation a plurality of persons may, in certain cases and conditions, preempt three hundred and twenty acres. In the latter contingency, there is no special privilege as to quantity, but a disability rather; for two persons together may preempt three hundred and twenty acres by agricultural occupation, and afterwards convert the land into a town site, and four persons together might in the same way secure six hundred and forty acres, to be converted ultimately into the site of a town; while the same four persons, selecting land for a town site, can take only three hundred and twenty acres. In both forms the parties enter at the minimum price of the public lands. The chief advantage which the preemptors for municipal purposes enjoy, is, that they have by statute a preference over agricultural preemptors, the land selected for a town site being secured by statute against general and ordinary, that is, agricultural preemption. In all other respects material to the present inquiry, we may assume, for the argument's sake at least, that the two classes stand on a footing of equality, as respects either the convicting interests of third persons, or the rights of the Government.

Now, the rights of an agricultural preemptor we understand. He is entitled, if he shall "make a settlement in person on the public lands," and "shall inhabit and improve the same, and shall erect a dwelling thereon," to enter, "by legal subdivisions, any number of acres not exceeding one hundred and sixty, or a quarter-section of land, to include the residence of such claimant." (Act of 1841, s. 10.) And of two settlers on "the same quarter-section of land," the earlier one is to have the preference. (Sec. 11.)

Now, was it ever imagined that such claimant must personally inhabit every quarter quarter-section of his claim? That he must have under cultivation every quarter quarter-section? That he must erect a dwelling on every quarter quarter-section? And that, if he failed to do this, any such quarter of his quarter-section might be preempted by a later occupant?

There is no pretension that such is the condition of the ordinary preemptor, and that he is thus held to inhabit, to cultivate, to dwell on, every quarter quarter-section, under penalty of having it seized by another preemptor, or entered in course by any public or private purchaser. He is to provide, according to the regulations of the Land Office or otherwise, indicia, by which the limits of his claim shall be known,— he must perform acts of possession or intended ownership on the land, as notice to others; and that suffices to secure his rights under the statute. It is not necessary for him to cultivate every separate quarter of his quarter-section; it is not necessary for him even to enclose each; it only needs that in good faith he take possession, with intention of occupation and settlement, and proceed in good faith to occupy and settle, in such time and in such manner, as belong to the nature of agricultural occupation and settlement.

Why should there be a different rule in regard to occupants for municipal preemption? The latter is, by the very tenor of the law, the preferred object. Why should those interested in it be subject to special disabilities of competing occupancy? I cannot conceive.

It is obvious that, in municipal settlement, as well as agricultural, there must be space of time between the commencement and the consummation of occupation. There will be a moment, when the equitable right of the agricultural settler is fixed, although he have as yet done nothing more in the way of inhabiting or improving than to cut a tree or drive a stake into the earth. And it may be long before he improves each one of all his quarter quarter-sections. So, in principle, it is in the case of settlement for a town. We must deal with such things according to their nature. Towns do not spring into existence consummate and complete. Nor do they commence with eight houses, systematically distributed, each in the centre of a forty-acre lot. And in the case of a town settlement of three hundred and twenty acres; as well as that of a farm site of one hundred and sixty acres, all which can be lawfully requisite to communicate to the occupants the right of preemption to the block of land, including every one of its quarter quarter-sections, — is improvement, or indication of the improvement of the entire block, — acts of possession or use regarding it, consonant with the nature of the thing. That, in a farm, will be the erection of a house and outhouses, cultivation, and use of pasturage or woodland: in a town, it will be erecting houses or shops, platting out the land, grading or opening streets, and the like signs and marks of occupation or special destination.

The same considerations lead to the conclusion that it would not be just to confine the proofs of occupation to facts existing at its very incipiency. The inchoate or equitable right, as against all others, begins from the beginning of the occupation: the ultimate sufficiency of that occupation is to be determined in part by subsequent facts, which consummate the occupation, and also demonstrate its *bona fides.* If it were otherwise, there would be an end of all the advantage expressly given by the statute to priority of occupation. Take the case of agricultural preemptions for example. A settler enters in good faith upon a quarter-section for preemption; his entry, at first, attaches physically to no more than the rood of land on which he is commencing to construct a habitation. Is that entry confined in effect to a single *quarter* quarter? Can other settlers, the next day, enter upon all the adjoining quarter quarters, and thus limit the first settler to the single quarter quarter on which his dwelling is commenced? Is all proof of occupation in his case, when he comes to prove up his title, to be confined to acts anterior to the date of conflict? Clearly not. The inchoate title of the first occupant ripens into a complete one by the series of acts on his part subsequent to the original occupation.

In the statement of the case prepared in your office, it is averred that numerous precedents exist in the Land Office, not only of the allowance of town preemptions as the voluntary selection of individuals, but also of the application to such preemption claims of the ordinary construction of the word "occupation" habitually applied to agricultural preemption claims. That is to say, it has been the practice of the Government, not to consider municipal occupation "circumscribed by the forty-acre subdivisions actually built upon; * *

158

but that such occupation was (sufficiently) evidenced, either by an actual survey, upon the ground, of said town into streets, alleys, and blocks, or the publication of a plat of the same evidencing the connection therewith of the public surveys, so as to give notice to others of the extent of the town site:" all this, within the extreme limits, of course, of the three hundred and twenty acres prescribed by the statute.

I think the practice of the Land Office in this respect, as thus reported, is lawful and proper: it being understood, of course, that thus the acts of alleged selection, possession, and occupation are performed in perfect good faith.

Something is hinted, in the report of the commissioner, as to the speculation-character of the proposed town settlement, — and, in the official brief accompanying your letter, as to the speculation-character of the proposed agricultural preemption. I suppose it must be so, if the land in question has peculiar aptitude for municipal uses. But how is that material? The object, in either mode of attaining it, is a lawful one. Two persons may lawfully preempt a certain quantity of land under the general law, and *intend* a townsite without saying so; or they may preempt *avowedly* for a town site. As between the two courses, both having the same ultimate destination, it would not seem that there could be any cause of objection to the more explicit one.

So much for the first branch of the second question. As to the second branch of it, the same line of reasoning leads to equally satisfactory results.

The municipal preemptor, like the agricultural preemptor, is required to take his land in conformity with "the legal subdivisions of the public lands." I apprehend the import of the requirement is the same in both cases. Neither class of pre-emptors is to break the legal subdivisions as surveyed. The preemptor of either case may take fractional sections if he will, but he is in every case to run his extreme lines with the lines of the surveyed subdivisions. In fine, as it seems to me, there is nothing of the present case, in so far as appears by the questions presented, and the official reports and statement by which they are explained, except a convict of claim to two or three sectional subdivisions of land between different sets of preemptors, one set being avowed municipal preemptors, and the other professed agricultural preemptors, but both sets having in reality the same ulterior purposes in regard to the use of the land. The Government has no possible concern in the controversy, except to deal impartially between the parties according to law. The agricultural preemptors contend that different rules of right as to the power of individual or private occupation, and as to the *criteria* of valid occupation, apply to them, as against their adversaries. The municipal preemptors contend that the same rules of equal right, inceptive and progressive, in these respects, apply to both classes of preemptors. I think that the latter view of the law is correct, according to its letter, its spirit; and the settled practice of the Government.

The investigation of the facts of the case, and the application of the law to the facts, are, of course, duties of your Department.

I leave here the first and second questions; and, proposing to reply at an early day on the third question,

I have the honor to be, very respectfully,

C. CUSHING.

Hon. ROBERT McCLELLAND,

Secretary of the *Interior.*

THE END.

ADVERTISEMENT.

THE OFFICIAL OPINIONS OF THE. ATTORNEYS GENERAL OF THE UNITED STATES. Edited by C. C. ANDREWS, Esq. VOLUME VII. (8 vo.) now ready. Washington: Published by R. Farnham.

"In this series the proudest names of American law have found some appropriate record of their labor and their wisdom. * * No student of the law can find more valuable reading than in these opinions. We would urge upon him to turn now and then from the common place reading of the profession to the great studies which impart, to the law the dignity of a science. If less immediate in the rewards they bring, they are the only studies which can win for the legal aspirant the true glory of a great lawyer."— *Monthly Law Reporter*.

"Mr. Andrews is entitled to the thanks of his professional brethren for the very satisfactory manner in which he has presented these opinions."— American Law *Register*.

"On such examination as I have been able to give it (Volume VI.), the volume seems to me to be full of instruction; the argument most clearly and fairly conducted; the researches thorough, and the conclusions, in so far as I can form a judgment, just."— *Rufus Choate*.

"But we should fail entirely in our object, of calling attention to this work if we did not particularly commend it to the notice of the statesman and the general reader. * * These volumes constitute a great treatise on constitutional law; the work, not of one man, but of a succession of able men from the age of Washington, who have examined and revised each other. We regard it, therefore, as one of the most valuable publications which has embellished our political and legal literature."— *National Intelligencer*.

A TREATISE ON THE REVENUE LAWS OF THE UNITED STATES, in one volume, 8 vo. By C. C. ANDREWS, Esq. (Soon to be published by Little, Brown and Company. See their list of new Law Books.)

REFLECTIONS ON THE OPERATION OF THE PRESENT SYSTEM OF EDUCATION. By C. C. ANDREWS, Esq. Boston: Crosby, Nichols and Company: 1853.

"The substance of the pamphlet appeared some time since in a monthly journal, and the author has now revised it and published it in a more permanent form. His views are sensible, and well deserve attention."— *BostonDaily Advertiser*.

"This is an earnest and well written essay; designed to remedy what the writer justly regards an important defect in the present system of education-namely, the want of a proper degree of moral instruction. His observations evince an enlightened mind, as well as a philanthropic spirit; and they deserve to be considerately pondered by all whom they may concern."— *Puritan Recorder*.

"His practical remarks are of particular value, and show that the author has devoted much thought to the topic of which he treats." — *Boston Daily Atlas.*

"We have perused this publication with more than ordinary interest. The object of the author is to suggest some remedies for the acknowledged defects in the operation of our system of education. This object is pursued by a masterly hand, in a lucid and comprehensive manner." — *Evening Transcript.*

"This contribution to the cause of common school education is highly creditable to the author, and we have no doubt, if it can be extensively circulated, will be productive of very beneficial results." — *Christian Witness.*